T0020055

Birds *of*
Washington

Field Guide

Stan Tekiela

Adventure Publications
Cambridge, Minnesota

Dedication

To my wife, Katherine, and daughter, Abigail, with all my love

Acknowledgments

Special thanks to the National Wildlife Refuge System, which stewards the land that is critical to many bird species.

Edited by Sandy Livoti and Dan Downing

Cover, book design and illustrations by Jonathan Norberg

Range maps produced by Anthony Hertzel

Cover photo: Spotted Towhee by Stan Tekiela
All photos by Stan Tekiela except p. 256 by **Agami Photo Agency/Shutterstock**; pp. 86, 334 (non-breeding male) by **Paul Bannick**; pp. 76 (inset), 110 (female), 138 (both), 290 (both), 292 (both), 308 (juvenile), 322 (female), 334 (female), 336 (both) by **Rick & Nora Bowers**; pp. 208 (chick-feeding adult & juvenile), 306 (breeding), 310 (in flight) by **Dudley Edmondson**; pp. 212 (female), 312 (winter) by **Kevin T. Karlson**; p. 274 (female) by **Thomas Morris/Shutterstock**; p. 230 by **Laura Mountain-spring/Shutterstock**; p. 126 by **Nick Pecker/Shutterstock**; pp. 126 (winter), 142 (breeding), 238 (breeding), 306 (winter), 310 (juvenile & winter), 312 (breeding & in flight) by **Brian E. Small**; p. 84 (female) by **Sundry Photography/Shutterstock**; pp. 122 (female), 300 (female) by **vagabond54/Shutterstock**; pp. 42 (juvenile), 152 (juvenile & in-flight juvenile), 192 (dark morph, intermediate morph & soaring dark morph), 204 (juvenile), 258 (juvenile), 260 (in-flight juvenile) by **Brian K. Wheeler**; pp. 122 (male), 300 (male) by **wildphoto3/Shutterstock**; p. 228 (female) by **Greg A Wilson/Shutterstock**; p. 88 by **yhelfman/Shutterstock**; and pp. 188 (female), 236 (brown morph), 252 (main), 262 (female), 326 (female) by **Jim Zipp**.

To the best of the publisher's knowledge, all photos were of live birds. Some were photographed in a controlled condition.

10 9 8 7 6 5 4 3 2

Birds of Washington Field Guide
First Edition 2001
Second Edition 2022
Copyright © 2001 and 2022 by Stan Tekiela
Published by Adventure Publications
An imprint of AdventureKEEN
310 Garfield Street South
Cambridge, Minnesota 55008
(800) 678-7006
www.adventurepublications.net
All rights reserved
Printed in China
ISBN 978-1-64755-154-4 (pbk.); ISBN 978-1-64755-155-1 (ebook)

TABLE OF CONTENTS

WHAT'S NEW?

It is hard to believe that it's been more than 20 years since the debut of *Birds of Washington Field Guide*. This critically acclaimed field guide has helped countless people identify and enjoy the birds that we love. Now, in this expanded second edition, *Birds of Washington Field Guide* has many new and exciting changes and a fresh look, while retaining the same familiar, easy-to-use format.

To help you identify even more birds in Washington, I have added 8 new species and more than 150 new color photographs. All of the range maps have been meticulously reviewed, and many updates have been made to reflect the ever-changing movements of the birds.

Everyone's favorite section, "Stan's Notes," has been expanded to include even more natural history information. "Compare" sections have been updated to help ensure that you correctly identify your bird, and additional feeder information has been added to help with bird feeding. I hope you will enjoy this great new edition as you continue to learn about and appreciate our Washington birds!

WHY WATCH BIRDS IN WASHINGTON?

Millions of people have discovered bird feeding. It's a simple and enjoyable way to bring the beauty of birds closer to your home. Watching birds at your feeder often leads to a lifetime pursuit of bird identification. The *Birds of Washington Field Guide* is for those who want to identify common birds of Washington.

There are over 1,100 species of birds found in North America. In Washington alone there have been over 440 different kinds of birds recorded throughout the years. These bird sightings were diligently recorded by hundreds of bird watchers and became part of the official state record. From these valuable records, I've chosen 138 of the most common birds of Washington to include in this field guide.

Bird watching, often called birding, is one of the most popular activities in America. Its outstanding appeal in Washington is due, in part, to an unusually rich and abundant birdlife. Why are there so many birds? One reason is open space. Washington is over 70,000 square miles (182,200 sq. km), making it the nineteenth largest state. Despite its size, only about 7.5 million people call Washington home. On average, that's only 107 people per square mile (41 per sq. km). Most of these people are located along the Pacific. Over half of the population lives around Puget Sound. This concentration of people leaves plenty of room for birds.

Water, both saltwater and fresh, plays a big part in Washington's bird populations as well. Washington has more than 157 miles (253 km) of coastline, which is home to many ocean-loving birds such as the Double-crested Cormorant and California Gull. In addition to the Pacific coast, Washington has many freshwater and saltwater marshes, not to mention several major rivers, most of which drain into the ocean. All of this water attracts millions of birds such as the American Wigeon and Blue-winged Teal.

Open space and water are not the only reasons there is such an abundance of birds. It's also the diversity of habitat. Washington can be broken into four distinct habitats—Pacific Border, Sierra-Cascade Mountains, Columbia Plateau and the Northern Rocky Mountains—each of which supports a different group of birds.

The Pacific Border province occupies the western portion of the state and includes the entire length of Washington's coastline. It also encompasses the Washington Coast Ranges, consisting of the Olympic Mountains and Willapa Hills, which are home to birds such as the Chestnut-backed Chickadee and Band-tailed Pigeon. This coastal province is also the best place to see many water birds such as the Lesser Scaup and wintering Dunlin.

The Sierra-Cascade province is dominated by the Cascade Range and its tallest peak, Mount Rainier. Paralleling the Pacific Border province, running almost due north and south through central Washington, this area is home to the Rufous Hummingbird and Downy Woodpecker.

The Columbia Plateau lies in the southeastern part of the state. It is a rolling, prairie-like region with heavy agricultural activity (wheat). This locale is home to open-country birds such as the Horned Lark, and Eastern and Western Kingbirds.

In the northeastern quarter of the state are the Northern Rocky Mountains, the fourth physiographic region, with such birds as the Violet-green Swallow and Mountain Chickadee.

Varying habitats in Washington also mean variations in weather. Since elevation in the state rises from sea level along the coast to over 14,000 feet (4,250 m) at Mount Rainier, the state's highest peak, there are great differences in the weather.

Tall peaks in the Cascade Mountains are some of the coldest and snowiest places in Washington, while the Columbia Plateau in the southeast is the beneficiary of warming air as it moves down from the high country. Diversity of weather is another reason why Washington is a great place to see a wide variety of birds.

OBSERVE WITH A STRATEGY: TIPS FOR IDENTIFYING BIRDS

Identifying birds isn't as difficult as you might think. By simply following a few basic strategies, you can increase your chances of successfully identifying most birds that you see. One of the first and easiest things to do when you see a new bird is to note **its color**. This field guide is organized by color, so simply turn to the right color section to find it.

Next, note the **size of the bird.** A strategy to quickly estimate size is to compare different birds. Pick a small, a medium and a large bird. Select an American Robin as the medium bird. Measured from bill tip to tail tip, a robin is 10 inches (25 cm). Now select two other birds, one smaller and one larger. Good choices are a House Sparrow, at about 6 inches (15 cm), and an American Crow, around 18 inches (45 cm). When you see a species you don't know, you can now quickly ask yourself, "Is it larger than a sparrow but smaller than a robin?" When you look in your field guide to identify your bird, you would check the species that are roughly 6–10 inches (15–25 cm). This will help to narrow your choices.

Next, note the **size, shape and color of the bill.** Is it long or short, thick or thin, pointed or blunt, curved or straight? Seed-eating birds, such as Evening Grosbeaks, have bills that are thick and strong enough to crack even the toughest seeds. Birds that sip nectar, such as Broad-tailed Hummingbirds, need long, thin bills to reach deep into flowers. Hawks and owls tear their prey with very sharp, curving bills. Sometimes, just noting the bill shape can help you decide whether the bird is a woodpecker, finch, grosbeak, blackbird or bird of prey.

Next, take a look around and note the **habitat** in which you see the bird. Is it wading in a saltwater marsh? Walking along a riverbank or on the beach? Soaring in the sky? Is it perched high in the trees or hopping along the forest floor? Because of diet and habitat preferences, you'll often see robins hopping on the ground but not usually eating seeds at a feeder. Or you'll see a Steller's Jay sitting on a tree branch but not climbing headfirst down the trunk, like a Red-breasted Nuthatch would.

Noticing **what the bird is eating** will give you another clue to help you identify the species. Feeding is a big part of any bird's life. Fully one-third of all bird activity revolves around searching for food, catching prey and eating. While birds don't always follow all the rules of their diet, you can make some general assumptions. Northern Flickers, for instance, feed on ants and other insects, so you wouldn't expect to see them visiting a seed feeder. Other birds, such as Barn and Cliff Swallows, eat flying insects and spend hours swooping and diving to catch a meal.

Sometimes you can identify a bird by **the way it perches.** Body posture can help you differentiate between an American Crow and a Red-tailed Hawk, for example. Crows lean forward over their feet on a branch, while hawks perch in a vertical position. Consider posture the next time you see an unidentified large bird in a tree.

Birds in flight are harder to identify, but noting the **wing size and shape** will help. Wing size is in direct proportion to body size, weight and type of flight. Wing shape determines whether the bird flies fast and with precision, or slowly and less precisely. Barn Swallows, for instance, have short, pointed wings that slice through the air, enabling swift, accurate flight. Turkey Vultures have long, broad wings for soaring on warm updrafts. House Finches have short, rounded wings, helping them to flit through thick tangles of branches.

Some bird species have a unique **pattern of flight** that can help in identification. American Goldfinches fly in a distinctive undulating pattern that makes it look like they're riding a roller coaster.

While it's not easy to make all of these observations in the short time you often have to watch a "mystery" bird, practicing these identification methods will greatly expand your birding skills. To further improve your skills, seek the guidance of a more experienced birder who can answer your questions on the spot.

BIRD BASICS

It's easier to identify birds and communicate about them if you know the names of the different parts of a bird. For instance, it's more effective to use the word "crest" to indicate the set of extra-long feathers on top of the head of a Steller's Jay than to try to describe it. The following illustration points out the basic parts of a bird. Because it is a composite of many birds, it shouldn't be confused with any actual bird.

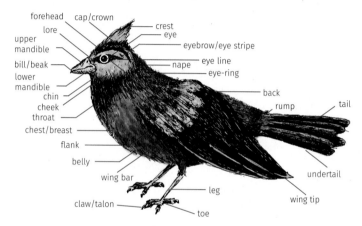

Bird Color Variables

No other animal has a color palette like a bird's. Brilliant blues, lemon yellows, showy reds and iridescent greens are common in the bird world. In general, male birds are more colorful than their female counterparts. This helps males attract a mate, essentially saying, "Hey, look at me!" Color calls attention to a male's health as well. The better the condition of his feathers, the better his food source, territory and potential for mating.

Male and female birds that don't look like each other are called sexually dimorphic, meaning "two forms." Dimorphic females often have a nondescript dull color, as seen in Lazuli Buntings. Muted tones help females hide during the weeks of motionless incubation and draw less attention to them when they're out feeding or taking a break from the rigors of raising the young.

The males of some species, such as the Downy Woodpecker, Steller's Jay and Bald Eagle, look nearly identical to the females. In woodpeckers, the sexes are differentiated by only a red mark, or sometimes a yellow mark. Depending on the species, the mark may be on top of the head, on the face or nape of neck, or just behind the bill.

During the first year, juvenile birds often look like their mothers. Since brightly colored feathers are used mainly for attracting a mate, young non-breeding males don't have a need for colorful plumage. It's not until the first spring molt (or several years later, depending on the species) that young males obtain their breeding colors.

Both breeding and winter plumages are the result of molting. Molting is the process of dropping old, worn feathers and replacing them with new ones. All birds molt, typically twice a year, with the spring molt usually occurring in late winter. At this time, most birds produce their brighter breeding plumage, which lasts throughout the summer.

Winter plumage is the result of the late summer molt, which serves a couple of important functions. First, it adds feathers for warmth in the coming winter season. Second, in some species it produces feathers that tend to be drab in color, which helps to camouflage the birds and hide them from predators. The winter plumage of the male American Goldfinch, for example, is olive-brown, unlike its canary-yellow breeding color during summer. Luckily for us, some birds, such as the Lewis's Woodpecker, retain their bright summer colors all year long.

Bird Nests

Bird nests are a true feat of engineering. Imagine constructing a home that's strong enough to weather storms, large enough to hold your entire family, insulated enough to shelter them from cold and heat, and waterproof enough to keep out rain. Think about building it without blueprints or directions and using mainly your feet. Birds do this!

Before building, birds must select an appropriate site. In some species, such as the House Wren, the male picks out several potential sites and assembles small twigs in each. The "extra" nests, called dummy nests, discourage other birds from using any nearby cavities for their nests. The male takes the female around and shows her the choices. After choosing her favorite, she finishes the construction.

In other species, such as the Bullock's Oriole, the female selects the site and builds the nest, while the male offers an occasional suggestion. Each bird species has its own nest-building routine that is strictly followed.

As you can see in these illustrations, birds build a wide variety of nest types.

| **ground nest** | **platform nest** | **cup nest** | **pendulous nest** | **cavity nest** |

Nesting material often consists of natural items found in the immediate area. Most nests consist of plant fibers (such as bark from grapevines), sticks, mud, dried grass, feathers, fur, or soft, fuzzy tufts from thistle. Some birds, including Calliope Hummingbirds, use spiderwebs to glue nest materials together.

Transportation of nesting material is limited to the amount a bird can hold or carry. Birds must make many trips afield to gather enough material to complete a nest. Most nests take four days or more, and hundreds, if not thousands, of trips to build.

A **ground nest** can be a mound of vegetation on the ground or in the water. It can also be just a simple, shallow depression scraped out in earth, stones or sand. Killdeer and Horned Larks scrape out ground nests without adding any nesting material.

The **platform nest** represents a much more complex type of construction. Typically built with twigs or sticks and branches, this nest forms a platform and has a depression in the center to nestle the eggs. Platform nests can be in trees; on balconies, cliffs, bridges, or man-made platforms; and even in flowerpots. They often provide space for the adventurous young and function as a landing platform for the parents.

Mourning Doves and herons don't anchor their platform nests to trees, so these can tumble from branches during high winds and storms. Hawks, eagles, ospreys and other birds construct sturdier platform nests with large sticks and branches.

Other platform nests are constructed on the ground with mud, grass and other vegetation from the area. Many waterfowl build platform nests on the ground near or in water. A **floating platform nest** moves with the water level, preventing the nest, eggs and birds from being flooded.

Three-quarters of all songbirds construct a **cup nest,** which is a modified platform nest. The supporting platform is built first and attached firmly to a tree, shrub, or rock ledge or the ground. Next, the sides are constructed with grass, small twigs, bark or leaves, which are woven together and often glued with mud for added strength. The inner cup can be lined with down feathers, animal fur or hair, or soft plant materials and is contoured last.

The **pendulous nest** is an unusual nest that looks like a sock hanging from a branch. Attached to the end of small branches of trees, this unique nest is inaccessible to most predators and often waves wildly in a breeze.

Woven tightly with plant fibers, the pendulous nest is strong and watertight and takes up to a week to build. A small opening at the top or on the side allows parents access to the grass-lined interior. More commonly used by tropical birds, this complex nest has also been mastered by orioles and kinglets. It must be one heck of a ride to be inside one of these nests during a windy spring thunderstorm!

The **cavity nest** is used by many species of birds, most notably woodpeckers and Western Bluebirds. A cavity nest is often excavated from a branch or tree trunk and offers shelter from storms, sun, cold and predators. A small entrance hole in a tree can lead to a nest chamber that is up to a safe 10 inches (25 cm) deep.

Typically made by woodpeckers, cavity nests are usually used only once by the builder. Nest cavities can be used for many subsequent years by such inhabitants as Wood Ducks, mergansers and bluebirds. Kingfishers, on the other hand, can dig a tunnel up to 4 feet (1 m) long in a riverbank. The nest chamber at the end of the tunnel is already well insulated, so it's usually only sparsely lined.

One of the most clever of all nests is the **no nest,** or daycare nest. Parasitic birds, such as Brown-headed Cowbirds, don't build their own nests. Instead, the egg-laden female searches out the nest of another bird and sneaks in to lay an egg while the host mother isn't looking.

A mother cowbird wastes no energy building a nest only to have it raided by a predator. Laying her eggs in the nests of other birds transfers the responsibility of raising her young to the host. When she lays her eggs in several nests, the chances increase that at least one of her babies will live to maturity.

Who Builds the Nest?

Generally, the female bird constructs the nest. She gathers the materials and does the building, with an occasional visit from her mate to check on progress. In some species, both parents contribute equally to nest building. The male may forage for sticks, grass or mud, but it is the female that often fashions the nest. Only rarely does a male build a nest by himself.

Fledging

Fledging is the time between hatching and flight, or leaving the nest. Some species of birds are **precocial,** meaning they leave the nest within hours of hatching, though it may be weeks before they can fly. This is common in waterfowl and shorebirds.

Baby birds that hatch naked and blind need to stay in the nest for a few weeks (these birds are **altricial**). Baby birds that are still in the nest are **nestlings.** Until birds start to fly, they are called **fledglings.**

Why Birds Migrate

Why do so many species of birds migrate? The short answer is simple: food. Birds migrate to locations with abundant food, as it is easier to breed where there is food than where food is scarce. Western Tanagers, for instance, are **complete migrators** that fly from the tropics of South America to nest in the forests of North America, where billions of newly hatched insects are available to feed to their young.

Other migrators, such as some birds of prey, migrate back to northern regions in spring. In these locations, they hunt mice, voles and other small rodents that are beginning to breed.

Complete migrators have a set time and pattern of migration. Every year at nearly the same time, they head to a specific wintering ground. Complete migrators may travel great distances, sometimes 15,000 miles (24,100 km) or more in one year.

Complete migration doesn't necessarily imply flying from the cold, frozen northland to a tropical destination. The Dark-eyed Junco, for example, is a complete migrator that flies from the far reaches of Canada to spend the winter right here in Washington. This trip is still considered complete migration.

Complete migrators have many interesting aspects. In spring, males often leave a few weeks before the females, arriving early to scope out possibilities for nesting sites and food sources, and to begin to defend territories. The females arrive several weeks later. In many species, the females and their young leave earlier in the fall, often up to four weeks before the adult males.

Other species, such as the Lesser Goldfinch, are **partial migrators**. These birds usually wait until their food supplies dwindle before flying south. Unlike complete migrators, partial migrators move only far enough south, or sometimes east and west, to find abundant food. In some years it might be only a few hundred miles, while in other years it can be as much as a thousand. This kind of migration, dependent on weather and the availability of food, is sometimes called seasonal movement.

Unlike the predictable complete migrators or partial migrators, **irruptive migrators** can move every third to fifth year or, in some cases, in consecutive years. These migrations are triggered when times are tough and food is scarce. Red-breasted Nuthatches are irruptive migrators. They leave their normal northern range in search of more food or in response to overpopulation.

Many other birds don't migrate at all. Black-capped Chickadees, for example, are **non-migrators** that remain in their habitat all year long and just move around as necessary to find food.

How Do Birds Migrate?

One of the many secrets of migration is fat. While most people are fighting the ongoing battle of the bulge, birds intentionally gorge themselves to gain as much fat as possible without losing the ability to fly. Fat provides the greatest amount of energy per unit of weight. In the same way that your car needs gas, birds are propelled by fat and stall without it.

During long migratory flights, fat deposits are used up quickly, and birds need to stop to refuel. This is when backyard bird feeding stations and undeveloped, natural spaces around our towns and cities are especially important. Some birds require up to 2–3 days of constant feeding to build their fat reserves before continuing their seasonal trip.

Many birds, such as most eagles, hawks, Ospreys, falcons and vultures, migrate during the day. Larger birds can hold more body fat, go longer without eating and take longer to migrate. These birds glide along on rising columns of warm air, called thermals, that hold them aloft while they slowly make their way north or south. They generally rest at night and hunt early in the morning before the sun has a chance to warm the land and create good soaring conditions. Daytime migrators use a combination of landforms, rivers, and the rising and setting sun to guide them in the right direction.

The majority of small birds, called **passerines,** migrate at night. Studies show that some use the stars to navigate. Others use the setting sun, and still others, such as pigeons, use Earth's magnetic field to guide them north or south.

While flying at night may not seem like a good idea, it's actually safer. First, there are fewer avian predators hunting for birds at night. Second, night travel allows time during the day to find food in unfamiliar surroundings. Third, wind patterns at night tend to be flat, or laminar. Flat winds don't have the turbulence of daytime winds and can help push the smaller birds along.

HOW TO USE THIS GUIDE

To help you quickly and easily identify birds, this field guide is organized by color. Refer to the color key on the first page, note the color of the bird, and turn to that section. For example, the Pileated Woodpecker is black and white with a red crest. Because the bird is mostly black-and-white, it will be found in the black-and-white section.

Each color section is also arranged by size, generally with the smaller birds first. Sections may also incorporate the average size in a range, which in some cases reflects size differences between male and female birds. Flip through the pages in the color section to find the bird. If you already know the name of the bird, check the index for the page number.

In some species, the male and female are very different in color. In others, the breeding and winter plumage colors differ. These species will have an inset photograph with a page reference and will be found in two color sections.

You will find a variety of information in the bird description sections. To learn more, turn to the sample on pp. 22–23.

Range Maps

Range maps are included for each bird. Colored areas indicate where the bird is frequently found. The colors represent the presence of a species during a specific season, not the density, or amount, of birds in the area. Green is used for summer, blue for winter, red for year-round and yellow for migration.

While every effort has been made to depict accurate ranges, these are constantly in flux due to a variety of factors. Changing weather, habitat, species abundance and availability of vital resources, such as food and water, can affect the migration and movement of local populations, causing birds to be found in areas that are atypical for the species. So please use the maps as intended—as general guides only.

female
p. 287

male

Common Name

YEAR-ROUND
SUMMER
MIGRATION
WINTER

Size: measurement is from head to tip of tail; wingspan may be listed as well

Male: brief description of the male bird; may include breeding, winter or other plumages

Female: brief description of the female bird, which is sometimes different from the male

Juvenile: brief description of the juvenile bird, which often looks like the adult female

Nest: kind of nest the bird builds to raise its young; who builds it; number of broods per year

Eggs: number of eggs you might expect to see in a nest; color and marking

Incubation: average days the parents spend incubating the eggs; who does the incubation

Fledging: average days the young spend in the nest after hatching but before they leave the nest; who does the most "childcare" and feeding

Migration: type of migrator: complete (seasonal, consistent), partial (seasonal, destination varies), irruptive (unpredictable, depends on the food supply) or non-migrator

Food: what the bird eats most of the time (e.g., seeds, insects, fruit, nectar, small mammals, fish) and whether it typically comes to a bird feeder

Compare: notes about other birds that look similar and the pages on which they can be found; may include extra information to aid in identification

Stan's Notes: Interesting natural history information. This could be something to look or listen for or something to help positively identify the bird. Also includes remarkable features.

female
p. 135

male

YEAR-ROUND
SUMMER

Brown-headed Cowbird
Molothrus ater

Size: 7½" (19 cm)

Male: Glossy black with a chocolate-brown head. Dark eyes. Pointed, sharp gray bill.

Female: dull brown with a pointed, sharp, gray bill

Juvenile: similar to female but with dull-gray plumage and a streaked chest

Nest: no nest; lays eggs in nests of other birds

Eggs: 5–7; white with brown markings

Incubation: 10–13 days; host bird incubates eggs

Fledging: 10–11 days; host birds feed the young

Migration: complete, to southern states; non-migrator in parts of Washington

Food: insects, seeds; will come to seed feeders

Compare: The male Red-winged Blackbird (p. 31) is slightly larger with red-and-yellow patches on upper wings. European Starling (p. 27) has a shorter tail.

Stan's Notes: Cowbirds are members of the blackbird family. Of approximately 750 species of parasitic birds worldwide, this is the only parasitic bird in Washington. Brood parasites lay their eggs in the nests of other birds, leaving the host birds to raise their young. Cowbirds are known to have laid their eggs in the nests of over 200 species of birds. While some birds reject cowbird eggs, most incubate them and raise the young, even to the exclusion of their own. Look for warblers and other birds feeding young birds twice their own size. Named "Cowbird" for its habit of following bison and cattle herds to feed on insects flushed up by the animals.

winter

breeding

European Starling
Sturnus vulgaris

YEAR-ROUND

Size: 7½" (19 cm)

Male: Glittering, iridescent purplish black in spring and summer; duller and speckled with white in fall and winter. Long, pointed, yellow bill in spring; gray in fall. Pointed wings. Short tail.

Female: same as male

Juvenile: similar to adults, with grayish-brown plumage and a streaked chest

Nest: cavity; male and female line cavity; 2 broods per year

Eggs: 4–6; bluish with brown markings

Incubation: 12–14 days; female and male incubate

Fledging: 18–20 days; female and male feed the young

Migration: non-migrator to partial migrator; some will move to southern states; moves around to find food in winter

Food: insects, seeds, fruit; visits seed or suet feeders

Compare: The male Brown-headed Cowbird (p. 25) has a brown head. Look for the shiny, dark feathers to help identify the European Starling.

Stan's Notes: One of our most numerous songbirds. Mimics the songs of up to 20 bird species and imitates sounds, including the human voice. Jaws are more powerful when opening than when closing, enabling the bird to pry open crevices to find insects. Often displaces woodpeckers, chickadees and other cavity-nesting birds. Large families gather with blackbirds in the fall. Not a native bird; 100 starlings were introduced to New York City in 1890–91 from Europe. Bill changes color in spring and fall.

male

female

Spotted Towhee

Pipilo maculatus

YEAR-ROUND
SUMMER

Size: 8½" (22 cm)

Male: Mostly black with dirty-red-brown sides and a white belly. Multiple white spots on wings and sides. Long black tail with a white tip. Rich, red eyes.

Female: very similar to male but with a brown head

Juvenile: brown with a heavily streaked chest

Nest: cup; female builds; 1–2 broods per year

Eggs: 3–5; white with brown markings

Incubation: 12–14 days; female and male incubate

Fledging: 10–12 days; female and male feed young

Migration: partial migrator to non-migrator

Food: seeds, fruit, insects

Compare: Fox Sparrow (p. 129) is found in similar habitat, but it is brown and lacks the Spotted Towhee's white belly. American Robin (p. 245) is larger.

Stan's Notes: Found in a variety of habitats, from thick brush and chaparral to suburban backyards. Usually heard noisily scratching through dead leaves on the ground for food. Over 70 percent of its diet is plant material. Eats more insects during spring and summer. Well known to retreat from danger by walking away rather than taking to flight. Nest is nearly always on the ground under bushes but away from where the male perches to sing. Begins breeding in April. Lays eggs in May. After the breeding season, moves to higher elevations. Song and plumage vary geographically and aren't well studied or understood.

female
p. 145

male

YEAR-ROUND

Red-winged Blackbird
Agelaius phoeniceus

Size: 8½" (22 cm)

Male: Jet black with red-and-yellow patches (epaulets) on upper wings. Pointed black bill.

Female: heavily streaked brown with a pointed brown bill and white eyebrows

Juvenile: same as female

Nest: cup; female builds; 2–3 broods per year

Eggs: 3–4; bluish green with brown markings

Incubation: 10–12 days; female incubates

Fledging: 11–14 days; female and male feed the young

Migration: non-migrator to partial migrator; moves around in winter to find food

Food: seeds, insects; visits seed and suet feeders

Compare: The male Brown-headed Cowbird (p. 25) is smaller and glossier and has a brown head. The bold red-and-yellow epaulets distinguish the male Red-winged from other blackbirds.

Stan's Notes: One of the most widespread and numerous birds in Washington. Found around marshes, wetlands, lakes and rivers. Flocks with as many as 10,000 birds have been reported. Males arrive before the females and sing to defend their territory. The male repeats his call from the top of a cattail while showing off his red-and-yellow shoulder patches. The female chooses a mate and often builds her nest over shallow water in a thick stand of cattails. The male can be aggressive when defending the nest. Red-winged Blackbirds feed mostly on seeds in spring and fall, and insects throughout the summer.

31

male

female
p. 147

Brewer's Blackbird

Euphagus cyanocephalus

YEAR-ROUND
WINTER

Size: 9" (22.5 cm)

Male: Overall glossy black, shining green in direct light. Head more purple than green. Bright-white or pale-yellow eyes. Winter plumage can be dull gray to black.

Female: similar to male, only overall grayish brown, most have dark eyes

Juvenile: similar to female

Nest: cup; female builds; 1–2 broods per year

Eggs: 4–6; gray with brown markings

Incubation: 12–14 days; female incubates

Fledging: 13–14 days; female and male feed young

Migration: non-migrator to partial migrator

Food: insects, seeds, fruit

Compare: The male Brown-headed Cowbird (p. 25) is smaller and has a brown head. The male Red-winged Blackbird (p. 31) has red-and-yellow shoulder marks.

Stan's Notes: Common blackbird of open areas such as farms, wet pastures, mountain meadows and even desert scrub. Male and some females are easily identified by their bright, nearly white eyes. It is a common cowbird host, usually nesting in a shrub, small tree or directly on the ground. Prefers to nest in small colonies of up to 20 pairs. Gathers in large flocks with cowbirds, Red-wingeds and other blackbirds to migrate. It is expanding its range in North America.

female
p. 151

male

Yellow-headed Blackbird

Xanthocephalus xanthocephalus

SUMMER

Size:	9–11" (23–28 cm)
Male:	Large black bird with a lemon-yellow head, breast and nape of neck. Black mask and gray bill. White wing patches.
Female:	similar to male but slightly smaller with a brown body and dull-yellow head and chest
Juvenile:	similar to female
Nest:	cup; female builds; 2 broods per year
Eggs:	3–5; greenish white with brown markings
Incubation:	11–13 days; female incubates
Fledging:	9–12 days; female feeds the young
Migration:	complete, to southern states and Mexico
Food:	insects, seeds; will come to ground feeders
Compare:	The male Red-winged Blackbird (p. 31) is smaller and has red-and-yellow patches on its wings. Look for the bright-yellow head to identify the male Yellow-headed.

Stan's Notes: Found around marshes, wetlands and lakes. Nests in deep water, unlike its cousin, the Red-winged Blackbird, which prefers shallow water. Usually heard before seen. Gives a raspy, low, metallic-sounding call. The male is the only large black bird with a bright-yellow head. He gives an impressive mating display, flying with his head drooped and feet and tail pointing down while steadily beating his wings. Young keep low and out of sight for up to three weeks before they start to fly. Migrates in large flocks of as many as 200 birds, often with Red-winged Blackbirds and Brown-headed Cowbirds. Flocks of mainly males return first in late March and early April; females return later. Most colonies consist of 20–100 nests.

YEAR-ROUND
SUMMER

American Coot
Fulica americana

Size: 13–16" (33–40 cm)

Male: Gray-to-black waterbird. Duck-like white bill with a dark band near the tip and a small red patch near the eyes. Small white patch near base of tail. Green legs and feet. Red eyes.

Female: same as male

Juvenile: much paler than adults, with a gray bill

Nest: floating platform; female and male construct; 1 brood per year

Eggs: 9–12; pinkish buff with brown markings

Incubation: 21–25 days; female and male incubate

Fledging: 49–52 days; female and male feed young

Migration: partial migrator to complete, to western coastal U.S. and Mexico, Central America

Food: insects, aquatic plants

Compare: Smaller than most waterfowl, it is the only black, duck-like bird with a white bill.

Stan's Notes: Usually seen in large flocks on open water. Not a duck, as it has large lobed toes instead of webbed feet. An excellent diver and swimmer, bobbing its head as it swims. A favorite food of Bald Eagles. It is not often seen in flight, unless it's trying to escape from an eagle. To take off, it scrambles across the surface of the water, flapping its wings. Gives a unique series of creaks, groans and clicks. Anchors its floating platform nest to vegetation. Huge flocks with as many as 1,000 birds gather for migration. Migrates at night. The common name "Coot" comes from the Middle English word *coote*, which was used to describe various waterfowl. Also called Mud Hen.

in flight

YEAR-ROUND

American Crow
Corvus brachyrhynchos

Size: 18" (45 cm)

Male: All-black bird with black bill, legs and feet. Can have a purple sheen in direct sunlight.

Female: same as male

Juvenile: same as adult

Nest: platform; female builds; 1 brood per year

Eggs: 4–6; bluish to olive-green with brown marks

Incubation: 18 days; female incubates

Fledging: 28–35 days; female and male feed the young

Migration: non-migrator to partial migrator

Food: fruit, insects, mammals, fish, carrion; will come to seed and suet feeders

Compare: Common Raven (p. 41) is similar, but it has a larger bill and has shaggy throat feathers. Crow's call is higher than the raspy, low calls of ravens. Crow has a squared tail. Ravens have wedge-shaped tails, apparent in flight. Black-billed Magpie (p. 67) has a long tail and white belly.

Stan's Notes: One of the most recognizable birds in Washington, found in most habitats. Imitates other birds and human voices. One of the smartest of all birds and very social, often entertaining itself by provoking chases with other birds. Eats roadkill but is rarely hit by vehicles. Can live as long as 20 years. Often reuses its nest every year if it's not taken over by a Great Horned Owl. Unmated birds, known as helpers, help to raise the young. Extended families roost together at night, dispersing daily to hunt. Cannot soar on thermals; flaps constantly and glides downward. Gathers in huge communal flocks of up to 10,000 birds in winter.

in flight

Common Raven

Corvus corax

YEAR-ROUND

Size: 22–27" (56–69 cm)

Male: Large all-black bird with a shaggy beard of feathers on throat and chin. Large black bill. Large wedge-shaped tail, best seen in flight.

Female: same as male

Juvenile: same as adult

Nest: platform; female and male construct; 1 brood per year

Eggs: 4–6; pale green with brown markings

Incubation: 18–21 days; female incubates

Fledging: 38–44 days; female and male feed the young

Migration: non-migrator to partial migrator

Food: insects, fruit, small animals, carrion

Compare: American Crow (p. 39) is smaller and lacks the shaggy throat feathers. Glides on flat outstretched wings, compared to the slightly V-shaped pattern of the American Crow. Low raspy call, compared with the higher-pitched call of the American Crow.

Stan's Notes: Considered by some people to be the smartest of all birds. Known for its aerial acrobatics and long swooping dives. Soars on wind without flapping, like a raptor. Sometimes scavenges with crows and gulls. A cooperative hunter that often communicates the location of a good source of food to other ravens. Most start to breed at 3–4 years. Complex courtship includes grabbing bills, preening each other and cooing. Long-term pair bond. Uses the same nest site for many years.

soaring

juvenile

drying

Turkey Vulture

Cathartes aura

SUMMER
MIGRATION

Size: 26–32" (66–80 cm); up to 6' wingspan

Male: Large and black with a naked red head and legs. In flight, wings are two-toned with a black leading edge and a gray trailing edge. Wing tips end in finger-like projections. Tail is long and squared. Ivory bill.

Female: same as male but slightly smaller

Juvenile: similar to adults, with a gray-to-blackish head and bill

Nest: no nest or minimal nest, on a cliff or in a cave, sometimes in a hollow tree; 1 brood per year

Eggs: 1–3; white with brown markings

Incubation: 38–41 days; female and male incubate

Fledging: 66–88 days; female and male feed the young

Migration: complete, to southern states, Mexico and Central and South America

Food: carrion; parents regurgitate to feed the young

Compare: Bald Eagle (p. 75) is larger and lacks two-toned wings. Look for the obvious naked red head to identify the Turkey Vulture.

Stan's Notes: The naked head reduces the risk of feather fouling (picking up diseases) from contact with carcasses. It has a strong bill for tearing apart flesh. Unlike hawks and eagles, it has weak feet more suited for walking than grasping. One of the few birds with a developed sense of smell. Mostly mute, making only grunts and groans. Holds its wings in an upright V shape in flight. Teeters from wing tip to wing tip as it soars and hovers. Seen in trees with wings outstretched, sunning itself and drying after a rain.

in flight

juvenile

crests

drying

Double-crested Cormorant

Phalacrocorax auritus

YEAR-ROUND
SUMMER
MIGRATION

Size: 31–35" (79–89 cm); up to 4⅓' wingspan

Male: Large black waterbird with unusual blue eyes and a long, snake-like neck. Large gray bill, with yellow at the base and a hooked tip.

Female: same as male

Juvenile: lighter brown with a grayish chest and neck

Nest: platform; male and female construct; 1 brood per year

Eggs: 3–4; bluish white without markings

Incubation: 25–29 days; female and male incubate

Fledging: 37–42 days; male and female feed the young

Migration: partial migrator to non-migrator, to western coastal U.S.

Food: small fish, aquatic insects

Compare: The Turkey Vulture (p. 43) is similar in size and also perches on branches with wings open to dry in sun, but it has a naked red head. American Coot (p. 37) is half the size and lacks the Cormorant's long neck and long pointed bill.

Stan's Notes: Flocks fly in a large V or a line. Swims underwater to catch fish, holding its wings at its sides. This bird's outer feathers soak up water, but its body feathers don't. To dry off, it strikes an upright pose with wings outstretched, facing the sun. Gives grunts, pops and groans. Named "Double-crested" for the crests on its head, which are not often seen. "Cormorant" is a contraction from *corvus marinus*, meaning "crow" or "raven," and "of the sea."

male

female

Downy Woodpecker
Dryobates pubescens

YEAR-ROUND

Size: 6½" (15 cm)

Male: Small woodpecker with a white belly and black-and-white spotted wings. Red mark on the back of the head and a white stripe down the back. Short black bill.

Female: same as male but lacks the red mark

Juvenile: same as female, some with a red mark near the forehead

Nest: cavity with a round entrance hole; male and female excavate; 1 brood per year

Eggs: 3–5; white without markings

Incubation: 11–12 days; female incubates during the day, male incubates at night

Fledging: 20–25 days; male and female feed the young

Migration: non-migrator

Food: insects, seeds; visits seed and suet feeders

Compare: The Hairy Woodpecker (p. 55) is larger. Look for the Downy's shorter, thinner bill.

Stan's Notes: Abundant and widespread where trees are present. This is perhaps the most common woodpecker in the U.S. Stiff tail feathers help to brace it like a tripod as it clings to a tree. Like other woodpeckers, it has a long, barbed tongue to pull insects from tiny places. Mates drum on branches or hollow logs to announce territory, which is rarely larger than 5 acres (2 ha). Repeats a high-pitched "peek-peek" call. Nest cavity is wider at the bottom than at the top and is lined with fallen wood chips. Male performs most of the brooding. During winter, it will roost in a cavity. Doesn't breed in high elevations but often moves there in winter for food. Undulates in flight.

Red-breasted Sapsucker

Sphyrapicus ruber

YEAR-ROUND
SUMMER

Size: 8½" (22 cm)

Male: Black and white body, wings and tail. Belly is white to pale yellow. Red head, chest and nape. White mark over bill.

Female: similar to male

Juvenile: similar to adult, lacking any red

Nest: cavity; female and male build; 1–2 broods per year

Eggs: 3–7; white without markings

Incubation: 12–14 days; male and female incubate

Fledging: 25–29 days; male and female feed the young

Migration: non-migrator to partial migrator

Food: insects, tree sap, berries

Compare: Similar to the Red-naped Sapsucker (p. 51), which has a black chest, and black and white on the head. The Red-breasted is found in western Washington, while the Red-naped is seen in eastern Washington.

Stan's Notes: Most common sapsucker in western Washington. Most common in higher elevations, it is rare in residential areas or city parks. Will hybridize with Red-naped Sapsuckers in central Washington. An important species because their cavity nests are subsequently used by many cavity-nesting birds that don't excavate their own. Excavates nest cavities in dead or dying deciduous trees such as cottonwood, aspen, birch or willow. Drills a horizontal grid pattern of holes in deciduous trees, from which it drinks sap and eats the insects that are attracted to sap. Will also eat berries.

male

female

Red-naped Sapsucker
Sphyrapicus nuchalis

SUMMER
MIGRATION

Size: 8½" (22 cm)

Male: Black-and-white pattern on the back in two rows. Red forehead, chin and nape of neck.

Female: same as male, but has a white chin and more white on the back

Juvenile: brown version of adults, lacking any of the red markings

Nest: cavity; female and male excavate; 1 brood per year

Eggs: 3–7; pale white without markings

Incubation: 12–13 days; female and male incubate

Fledging: 25–29 days; female and male feed young

Migration: complete, to Mexico and Central America

Food: insects, tree sap; will visit feeders

Compare: Red-breasted Sapsucker (p. 49) is similar but has a red breast. The male Williamson's Sapsucker (p. 53) has a bright-yellow belly.

Stan's Notes: Found in eastern Washington. Hybridizes with Red-breasted Sapsuckers in central Washington. Closely related to the Yellow-bellied Sapsucker of the eastern U.S. Often associated with aspen, cottonwood and willow trees, nearly always nesting in aspen trees where they are present. Creates several horizontal rows of holes in a tree from which sap oozes. A wide variety of birds and animals use the sap wells that sapsuckers drill. Sapsuckers lap the sap and eat the insects that are also attracted to sap. Cannot suck sap as the name implies; instead, they lap it with their tongues. Some females lack the white chin that helps to differentiate the sexes.

male

female

Williamson's Sapsucker

Sphyrapicus thyroideus

SUMMER

Size: 9" (22.5 cm)

Male: More black than white with a red chin and bright-yellow belly. Bold white stripes just above and below the eyes. White rump and wing patches flash during flight.

Female: finely barred black-and-white back, a brown head, yellow belly and no wing patches

Juvenile: similar to female

Nest: cavity; male excavates; 1 brood per year

Eggs: 3–7; pale white without markings

Incubation: 12–14 days; male and female incubate

Fledging: 21–28 days; female and male feed young

Migration: complete, to Mexico and Central America

Food: insects, tree sap; will visit feeders

Compare: Male Williamson's is similar to Red-naped (p. 51) and Red-breasted (p. 49) Sapsuckers, both of which have white on the back and red on the head. Female Williamson's is similar to the Northern Flicker (p. 157), but Flicker has a gray head and brown-and-black back.

Stan's Notes: Largest sapsucker species with a striking difference between the male and female. Male drums early in spring to attract a mate and claim territory. Like the drumming of other sapsuckers, Williamson's drumming has an irregular cadence. Male excavates a new cavity each year, frequently in the same tree. Male does more incubating than the female. Occupies coniferous forests, foraging for insects and drilling uniform rows of holes from which tree sap oozes. Sap wells are nearly exclusively in conifers.

male

female

Hairy Woodpecker
Leuconotopicus villosus

YEAR-ROUND

Size: 9" (23 cm)

Male: Black-and-white woodpecker with a white belly. Black wings with rows of white spots. White stripe down the back. Long black bill. Red mark on the back of the head.

Female: same as male but lacks the red mark

Juvenile: grayer version of the female

Nest: cavity with an oval entrance hole; female and male excavate; 1 brood per year

Eggs: 3–6; white without markings

Incubation: 11–15 days; female incubates during the day, male incubates at night

Fledging: 28–30 days; male and female feed the young

Migration: non-migrator

Food: insects, nuts, seeds; comes to seed and suet feeders

Compare: Downy Woodpecker (p. 47) is much smaller and has a much shorter bill. Look for Hairy Woodpecker's long bill.

Stan's Notes: A common bird in wooded backyards. Announces its arrival with a sharp chirp before landing on feeders. Responsible for eating many destructive forest insects. Uses its barbed tongue to extract insects from trees. Tiny, bristle-like feathers at the base of the bill protect the nostrils from wood dust. Drums on hollow logs, branches or stovepipes in spring to announce territory. Prefers to excavate nest cavities in live trees. Excavates a larger, more-oval-shaped entrance than the round entrance hole of the Downy Woodpecker. Makes short flights from tree to tree.

female
p. 163

male

Bufflehead
Bucephala albeola

YEAR-ROUND
SUMMER
MIGRATION
WINTER

Size: 13–15" (33–38 cm)

Male: A small, striking duck with white sides and a black back. Greenish-purple head, iridescent in bright sun, with a large white head patch.

Female: brownish-gray with a dark-brown head and white cheek patch behind the eyes

Juvenile: similar to female

Nest: cavity; female lines an old woodpecker cavity; 1 brood per year

Eggs: 8–10; ivory-to-olive without markings

Incubation: 29–31 days; female incubates

Fledging: 50–55 days; female leads the young to food

Migration: complete, to southern states, Mexico and Central America; non-migrator in parts of Washington

Food: aquatic insects, crustaceans, mollusks

Compare: Male Hooded Merganser (p. 61) is larger and has rust-brown sides. Look for the large white bonnet-like patch on a greenish-purple head to help identify the male Bufflehead.

Stan's Notes: A small, common diving duck, almost always seen in small groups or with other duck species on rivers, ponds and lakes. Usually seen during migrations and winter, arriving in August and remaining in Washington the entire winter. Most commonly found in sheltered bays and coastal harbors, it is also found inland on rivers and lakes. Nests in vacant woodpecker holes. Unlike other ducks, the young stay in the nest for up to two days before they venture out with their mothers. The female is very territorial and remains with the same mate for many years.

female p. 171

male

YEAR-ROUND
SUMMER
WINTER

Lesser Scaup
Aythya affinis

Size: 16–17" (40–43 cm)

Male: Appears mostly black with bold white sides and a gray back. Chest and head look nearly black, but head appears purple with green highlights in direct sun. Bright-yellow eyes.

Female: overall brown with a dull-white patch at the base of a light-gray bill; yellow eyes

Juvenile: same as female

Nest: ground; female builds; 1 brood per year

Eggs: 8–14; olive-buff without markings

Incubation: 22–28 days; female incubates

Fledging: 45–50 days; female teaches the young to feed

Migration: complete, to western coastal U.S., southern states, Mexico, Central American, northern South America

Food: aquatic plants and insects

Compare: American Coot (p. 37) is smaller and lacks male Scaup's white sides. The white sides and gray back help identify the male Lesser Scaup.

Stan's Notes: A common diving duck. Often seen in large flocks on lakes and ponds. Submerges completely to feed on the bottom (unlike dabbling ducks, which tip forward to reach the bottom). Frequently seen in large flocks numbering in the thousands on area lakes and ponds, and along the coast in winter. When seen in flight, note the bold white stripe under the wings. A rare breeder in Washington, breeding north of the state through Alaska. Interesting baby-sitting arrangement in which the young form groups tended by one to three adult females.

female
p. 173

male

Hooded Merganser
Lophodytes cucullatus

YEAR-ROUND
SUMMER
MIGRATION
WINTER

Size: 16–19" (40–48 cm)

Male: Black and white with rust-brown sides. Crest "hood" raises to show a large white patch on each side of the head. Long, thin, black bill.

Female: brown and rust with ragged, rust-red "hair" and a long, thin, brown bill

Juvenile: similar to female

Nest: cavity; female lines an old woodpecker cavity or a nest box near water; 1 brood per year

Eggs: 10–12; white without markings

Incubation: 32–33 days; female incubates

Fledging: 71 days; female feeds the young

Migration: complete, to western coastal U.S. and Mexico; non-migrator in parts of Washington

Food: small fish, aquatic insects, crustaceans (especially crayfish)

Compare: Male Bufflehead (p. 57) is smaller than Hooded Merganser and has white sides. The male Wood Duck (p. 281) is similar in size, but it has a green head. The white patch on the head and rust-brown sides distinguish the male Hoodie.

Stan's Notes: A small diving bird of shallow ponds, sloughs, lakes and rivers, usually in small groups. Quick, low flight across the water, with fast wingbeats. Male has a deep, rolling call. Female gives a hoarse quack. Nests in wooded areas. Female will lay some eggs in the nests of other Hooded Mergansers or Wood Ducks, resulting in 20–25 eggs in some nests. Rarely, she shares a nest, sitting with a Wood Duck.

winter

breeding

American Avocet
Recurvirostra americana

SUMMER
MIGRATION

Size: 18" (45 cm)

Male: Black-and-white back, with a white belly. A long, thin upturned bill and long gray legs. Rusty-red head and neck during breeding season, gray in winter.

Female: similar to male, more strongly upturned bill

Juvenile: similar to adults, slight wash of rusty red on the neck and head

Nest: ground; female and male construct; 1 brood per year

Eggs: 3–5; light olive with brown markings

Incubation: 22–29 days; female and male incubate

Fledging: 28–35 days; female and male feed young

Migration: complete to southwestern states and Mexico

Food: insects, crustaceans, aquatic vegetation, fruit

Compare: Look for the obvious rusty red head of breeding Avocet and long upturned bill.

Stan's Notes: A handsome, long-legged bird that prefers shallow alkaline, saline or brackish water, it is well adapted to arid western U.S. conditions. Uses its upturned bill to sweep from side to side across mud bottoms in search of insects. Both the male and female have a brood patch to incubate eggs and brood their young. Nests in central Washington in loose colonies of up to 20 pairs; all members defend against intruders together.

male

female

Pileated Woodpecker
Dryocopus pileatus

YEAR-ROUND

Size: 19" (48 cm)

Male: Crow-size woodpecker with a black back and bright-red forehead, crest and mustache. Long gray bill. White leading edge of wings flashes brightly during flight.

Female: same as male but with a black forehead; lacks a red mustache

Juvenile: similar to adults but duller and browner

Nest: cavity; male and female excavate; 1 brood per year

Eggs: 3–5; white without markings

Incubation: 15–18 days; female incubates during the day, male incubates at night

Fledging: 26–28 days; female and male feed the young

Migration: non-migrator; moves around to find food in winter

Food: insects; will come to suet and peanut feeders

Compare: This bird is quite distinctive and unlikely to be confused with any others. Look for the bright-red crest and exceptionally large size to identify the Pileated Woodpecker.

Stan's Notes: Our largest woodpecker. The common name comes from the Latin *pileatus*, which means "wearing a cap." A relatively shy bird that prefers large tracts of woodland. Drums on hollow branches, chimneys and so forth to announce its territory. Excavates oval holes up to several feet long in tree trunks, looking for insects to eat. Large wood chips lie on the ground by excavated trees. Favorite food is carpenter ants. Feeds regurgitated insects to its young. Young emerge from the nest looking just like the adults.

Black-billed Magpie
Pica hudsonia

YEAR-ROUND

Size: 20" (50 cm)

Male: Large black-and-white bird with a very long tail and white belly. Iridescent green wings and tail in direct sunlight. Large black bill and legs. White wing patches flash in flight.

Female: same as male

Juvenile: same as adult, but has a shorter tail

Nest: modified pendulous; male and female build; 1 brood per year

Eggs: 5–8; green with brown markings

Incubation: 16–21 days; female incubates

Fledging: 25–29 days; female and male feed young

Migration: non-migrator; moves around in winter to find food

Food: insects, carrion, fruit, seeds

Compare: The contrasting black-and-white colors and the very long tail of the Black-billed Magpie distinguish it from the all-black American Crow (p. 39).

Stan's Notes: A wonderfully intelligent bird that is able to mimic dogs, cats and even people. Will often raid a barnyard dog dish for food. Feeds on a variety of food from roadkill to insects and seeds it collects from the ground. Easily identified by its bold black-and-white colors and long streaming tail. Travels in small flocks, usually family members, and tends to be very gregarious. Breeds in small colonies. Unusual dome nest (dome-shaped roof) deep within thick shrubs. Mates with same mate for several years. Prefers open fields with cattle or sheep, where it feeds on insects attracted to livestock.

rushing

weed dance

Western Grebe
Aechmophorus occidentalis

SUMMER
MIGRATION
WINTER

Size: 24" (60 cm)

Male: Long-necked, nearly all-black water bird. White chin, neck, chest and belly. Long greenish-yellow bill. Bright-red eyes. Dark crown extends around eyes to base of bill. In winter, becomes light gray around eyes.

Female: same as male

Juvenile: similar to adult

Nest: platform; female and male construct; 1 brood per year

Eggs: 3–4; bluish white with brown markings

Incubation: 20–23 days; female and male incubate

Fledging: 65–75 days; female and male feed young

Migration: complete, to western coastal U.S.

Food: fish, aquatic insects

Compare: A familiar long-necked water bird. Striking black-and-white plumage makes it hard to confuse with any other bird.

Stan's Notes: Well known for its unusual breeding dance, called rushing. Side by side with necks outstretched, mates spring to their webbed feet and dance across the water's surface (see inset). Often holds long stalks of water plants in bill when courting (weed dance, see inset). Its legs are positioned far back on the body, making it difficult to walk on ground. Shortly after choosing a large lake for breeding, it rarely flies until late in summer. Young ride on backs of adults, climbing on minutes after hatching. Nests in large colonies of up to 100 pairs on lakes with tall vegetation.

soaring

Osprey
Pandion haliaetus

Size: 21–24" (53–61 cm); up to 5½' wingspan

Male: Large eagle-like bird with a white chest, belly and head. Dark eye line. Nearly black back. Black "wrist" marks on the wings. Dark bill.

Female: same as male but slightly larger and with a necklace of brown streaks

Juvenile: similar to adults, with a light-tan breast

Nest: platform on a raised wooden platform, man-made tower or tall dead tree; female and male build; 1 brood per year

Eggs: 2–4; white with brown markings

Incubation: 32–42 days; female and male incubate

Fledging: 48–58 days; male and female feed the young

Migration: complete, to southern states, Mexico and Central and South America

Food: fish

Compare: The juvenile Bald Eagle (p. 75) is brown with white speckles. The adult Bald Eagle has an all-white head and tail. Look for the white belly and dark eye line to identify the Osprey.

Stan's Notes: The only species in its family, and the only raptor that plunges into water feetfirst to catch fish. Always near water. Can hover for a few seconds before diving. Carries fish in a head-first position for better aerodynamics. Wings angle back in flight. Often harassed by Bald Eagles for its catch. Gives a high-pitched, whistle-like call, often calling in flight as a warning. Mates have a long-term pair bond. May not migrate to the same wintering grounds. Was nearly extinct but is now doing well.

breeding

winter

Common Loon
Gavia immer

YEAR-ROUND
SUMMER
MIGRATION
WINTER

Size: 28–36" (71–91 cm)

Male: Checkerboard back, black head, white necklace. Deep-red eyes. Long, pointed black bill. Winter plumage has a gray body and bill.

Female: same as male

Juvenile: similar to winter plumage, but lacks red eyes

Nest: ground, usually at the shoreline; female and male build; 1 brood per year

Eggs: 2; olive-brown, occasionally brown markings

Incubation: 26–31 days; female and male incubate

Fledging: 75–80 days; female and male feed the young

Migration: complete, to western and southern coastal U.S. and Mexico; non-migrator in bay area

Food: fish, aquatic insects, crayfish, salamanders

Compare: The Double-crested Cormorant (p. 45) has a black chest and gray bill with a hooked tip and yellow at the base. Look for a checkerboard back to identify the Common Loon.

Stan's Notes: A winter resident on the coast beginning in October, lasting until March. Some non-breeding adults stay all summer. Hunts for fish by eyesight and prefers clear, clean lakes. A great swimmer, but its legs are set so far back that it has a hard time walking. "Loon" comes from the Scandinavian term *lom*, meaning "lame," for the awkward way it walks on land. Its wailing call suggests wild laughter, which led to the phrase "crazy as a loon." Also gives soft hoots. In the water, young ride on the backs of their parents for about 10 days. Adults perform distraction displays to protect the young. Very sensitive to disturbance during nesting and will abandon the nest.

soaring

juvenile

soaring juvenile

Bald Eagle

Haliaeetus leucocephalus

YEAR-ROUND
WINTER

Size: 31–37" (79–94 cm); up to 7½' wingspan

Male: White head and tail contrast sharply with the dark-brown-to-black body and wings. Large, curved yellow bill and yellow feet.

Female: same as male but larger

Juvenile: dark brown with white speckles and spots on the body and wings; gray bill

Nest: massive platform, usually in a tree; female and male build; 1 brood per year

Eggs: 2–3; off-white without markings

Incubation: 34–36 days; female and male incubate

Fledging: 75–90 days; female and male feed the young

Migration: partial to non-migrator in Washington

Food: fish, carrion, birds (mainly ducks)

Compare: The Golden Eagle (p. 205) and Turkey Vulture (p. 43) lack the white head and white tail of adult Bald Eagle. The juvenile Golden Eagle, with its white wrist marks and white base of tail, is similar to the juvenile Bald Eagle.

Stan's Notes: Nearly became extinct due to DDT poisoning and illegal killing. Returns to the same nest each year, adding more sticks and enlarging it to huge proportions, at times up to 1,000 pounds (450 kg). In their midair mating ritual, one eagle flips upside down and locks talons with another. Both tumble, then break apart to continue flight. Not uncommon for juveniles to perform this mating ritual even though they have not reached breeding age. Long-term pair bond but will switch mates when not successful at reproducing. Juveniles attain the white head and tail at 4–5 years of age.

female
p. 111

male

Lazuli Bunting
Passerina amoena

SUMMER

Size: 5½" (14 cm)

Male: A turquoise-blue head, neck, back and tail. Cinnamon chest with cinnamon extending down flanks slightly. White belly. Two bold white wing bars. Non-breeding male has a spotty blue head and back.

Female: overall grayish brown, warm-brown breast, a light wash of blue on wings and tail, gray throat, light-gray belly and 2 narrow white wing bars

Juvenile: similar to adult of the same sex

Nest: cup; female builds; 2–3 broods per year

Eggs: 3–5; pale blue without markings

Incubation: 11–13 days; female incubates

Fledging: 10–12 days; female and male feed young

Migration: complete, to Mexico

Food: insects, seeds

Compare: The Western Bluebird (p. 85) is larger, darker blue, has a darker-brown breast and lacks white wing bars.

Stan's Notes: Most common in shrublands in the eastern portion of the state. Doesn't like dense forests. Strong association with water such as rivers and streams. Gathers in small flocks and tends to move up in elevations after breeding to hunt for insects and look for seeds. Has increased in population and expanded its range over the last century. Males sing from short shrubs and scrubby areas to attract females. Each male has his own unique combination of notes to produce his "own" song. Young males often copy songs of older males in the area.

Tree Swallow
Tachycineta bicolor

SUMMER

Size: 5–6" (13–15 cm)

Male: Blue-green in spring, greener in fall. Changes color in direct sunlight. White from chin to belly. Long, pointed wing tips. Notched tail.

Female: similar to male but duller

Juvenile: gray brown with a white belly and a grayish breast band

Nest: cavity; female and male line a vacant wood-pecker cavity or nest box; 2 broods per year

Eggs: 4–6; white without markings

Incubation: 13–16 days; female incubates

Fledging: 20–24 days; female and male feed the young

Migration: complete, to Mexico and Central America

Food: insects

Compare: The Barn Swallow (p. 81) has a rusty belly and a long, deeply forked tail. Similar size as the Cliff Swallow (p. 113) and Violet-green Swallow (p. 277), but it lacks any tan-to-rust color of the Cliff Swallow and any emerald green of the Violet-green Swallow.

Stan's Notes: The first swallow species to return each spring. Most common along ponds, lakes and agricultural fields. Can be attracted to your yard with a nest box. Competes with Western and Mountain Bluebirds for cavities and nest boxes. Builds a grass nest within and will travel long distances, looking for dropped feathers for the lining. Watch for it playing and chasing after feathers. Flies with rapid wingbeats, then glides. Gives a series of gurgles and chirps. Chatters when upset or threatened. Eats many nuisance bugs. Gathers in large flocks to migrate.

Barn Swallow
Hirundo rustica

SUMMER

Size: 7" (18 cm)

Male: Sleek swallow. Blue-black back, cinnamon belly and reddish-brown chin. White spots on a long, deeply forked tail.

Female: same as male but with a whitish belly

Juvenile: similar to adults, with a tan belly and chin, and shorter tail

Nest: cup; female and male build; 2 broods per year

Eggs: 4–5; white with brown markings

Incubation: 13–17 days; female incubates

Fledging: 18–23 days; female and male feed the young

Migration: complete, to South America

Food: insects (prefers beetles, wasps, flies)

Compare: Tree Swallow (p. 79) has a white belly and chin and a notched tail. Cliff Swallow (p. 113) and Violet-green Swallow (p. 277) are smaller and lack a distinctive, deeply forked tail. Violet-green Swallow is green with a white face. Look for Barn Swallow's deeply forked tail.

Stan's Notes: Seen in wetlands, farms, suburban yards and parks. Of the seven swallow species regularly found in Washington, this is the only one with a deeply forked tail. Unlike other swallows, it rarely glides in flight. Usually flies low over land or water. Drinks as it flies, skimming water, or will sip water droplets on wet leaves. Bathes while flying through rain or sprinklers. Gives a twittering warble, followed by a mechanical sound. Builds a mud nest with up to 1,000 beak-loads of mud. Nests on barns and houses, under bridges and in other sheltered places. Often nests in colonies of 4–6 birds; sometimes nests alone.

male

female

Mountain Bluebird
Sialia currucoides

SUMMER

Size: 7" (18 cm)

Male: Overall sky-blue bird with a darker blue head, back, wings and tail. White lower belly. Thin black bill.

Female: similar to male, but paler with a nearly gray head and chest and a whitish belly

Juvenile: similar to adult of the same sex

Nest: cavity, old woodpecker cavity, wooden nest box; female builds; 1–2 broods per year

Eggs: 4–6; pale blue without markings

Incubation: 13–14 days; female incubates

Fledging: 22–23 days; female and male feed young

Migration: complete, to Arizona, California and Mexico

Food: insects, fruit

Compare: Western Bluebird (p. 85) is similar, but it is darker blue with a rusty-red chest.

Stan's Notes: Common in open mountainous country, nesting in the eastern two-thirds of the state. Main diet is insects. Often hovers just before diving to the ground to grab an insect. Due to conservation of suitable nesting sites (dead trees with cavities and man-made nest boxes), populations have increased dramatically. Like other bluebirds, Mountain Bluebirds take well to nest boxes and tolerate close contact with people. Female sits on baby birds (brood) for up to six days after the eggs hatch. Young imprint on their first nest box or cavity and then choose a similar type of box or cavity throughout their life. Any open field is a good place to look for Mountain Bluebirds.

male

female

SUMMER

Western Bluebird
Sialia mexicana

Size: 7" (18 cm)

Male: Deep blue head, neck, throat, back, wings and tail. Rusty red chest and flanks.

Female: similar to male, only duller with a gray head

Juvenile: similar to female, with a speckled chest

Nest: cavity, old woodpecker cavity, wooden nest box; female builds; 1–2 broods per year

Eggs: 4–6; pale blue without markings

Incubation: 13–14 days; female incubates

Fledging: 22–23 days; female and male feed young

Migration: complete migrator in Washington, to Arizona, California and Mexico

Food: insects, fruit

Compare: The Mountain Bluebird (p. 83) is similar but lacks the rusty-red breast. Male Lazuli Bunting (p. 77) is smaller and has white wing bars.

Stan's Notes: More common in western Washington. Found in a variety of habitats, from agricultural land to clear-cuts. Requires a cavity for nesting. Competes with starlings for nest cavities. Like the Mountain Bluebird, it uses nest boxes, which are responsible for the stable populations. Populations dropped during the mid-1900s but recovered due to the efforts of concerned people who put up nest boxes, providing much-needed habitats for nesting. A courting male will fly in front of the female, spread his wings and tail, and perch next to her. Often goes in and out of its nest box or cavity as if to say, "Look inside." Male may offer food to the female to establish a pair bond.

YEAR-ROUND

Steller's Jay
Cyanocitta stelleri

Size: 11" (28 cm)

Male: Dark-blue wings, tail and belly. Black head, nape and chest. Large, pointed black crest on head that can be lifted at will.

Female: same as male

Juvenile: similar to adult

Nest: cup; female and male construct; 1 brood per year

Eggs: 3–5; pale green with brown markings

Incubation: 14–16 days; female incubates

Fledging: 16–18 days; female and male feed the young

Migration: non-migrator

Food: insects, berries, seeds; will visit seed feeders

Compare: The California Scrub-Jay (p. 89) lacks Steller's all-black head and black crest. Canada Jay (p. 249) lacks any blue coloring or a crest.

Stan's Notes: Common resident of coniferous forests from sea level to timberline. Often found in suburban yards. Thought to mate for life, rarely dispersing far, usually breeding within 10 miles (16 km) of birthplace. Several subspecies found throughout the West. Pacific form (shown) that is found in Washington has a black crest and lacks any distinct white streaks on the head. Usually very bold where it comes in contact with people on a regular basis, such as at a campground. Often seen in small flocks consisting mainly of family members. Feeds on a wide variety of food, but seeds make up 70 percent of the diet. Will cache seeds and acorns for later consumption. Was named after the Arctic explorer Georg W. Steller, who is said to have have first recorded the bird on the coast of Alaska in 1741.

California Scrub-Jay
Aphelocoma californica

YEAR-ROUND

Size:	11" (28 cm)
Male:	Head, wings, tail and breast band are deep blue. Brownish patch on back. Chin, breast and belly are dull white. Very long tail.
Female:	same as male
Juvenile:	similar to adult, overall gray with light-blue wings and tail
Nest:	cup; female and male build; 1 brood a year
Eggs:	3–6; pale green with red brown markings
Incubation:	15–17 days; female incubates
Fledging:	18–20 days; female and male feed the young
Migration:	non-migrator
Food:	insects, seeds, fruit; comes to seed feeders
Compare:	Same size as Steller's Jay (p. 87), but it lacks the all-black head and pointed crest. Canada Jay (p. 249) is gray and white, lacking any of the Scrub-Jay's blue color.

Stan's Notes: A tame bird of urban areas that visits feeders. Forms a long-term pair bond. The male feeds the female before and during incubation. Young of a pair remain close by for up to a couple years, helping parents raise subsequent siblings. Caches food by burying it for later consumption. Likely serves as a major distributor of oaks and pines by not returning to eat the seeds it buried. Was once called the Western Scrub Jay. Now broken into two separates species, the California Scrub-Jay and the Woodhouse's Scrub-Jay. The California Scrub-Jay occurs in Washington and Oregon, while Woodhouse's is found in Idaho and other Rocky Mountain states.

89

Belted Kingfisher
Megaceryle alcyon

YEAR-ROUND

Size: 12–14" (30–36 cm)

Male: Blue with white belly, blue-gray chest band, and black wing tips. Ragged crest moves up and down at will. Large head. Long, thick, black bill. White spot by eyes. Red-brown eyes.

Female: same as male but with rusty flanks and a rusty chest band below the blue-gray band

Juvenile: similar to female

Nest: cavity; female and male excavate in a bank of a river, lake or cliff; 1 brood per year

Eggs: 6–7; white without markings

Incubation: 23–24 days; female and male incubate

Fledging: 23–24 days; female and male feed the young

Migration: non-migrator in Washington; moves around to find food in winter

Food: small fish

Compare: Larger than the California Scrub-Jay (p. 89), which lacks Kingfisher's obvious large crest. The Belted Kingfisher is rarely found away from water.

Stan's Notes: Usually found at the bank of a river, lake or large stream. Perches on a branch near water, dives in headfirst to catch a small fish, then returns to the branch to feed. Parents drop dead fish into the water to teach their young to dive. Can't pass bones through its digestive tract; regurgitates bone pellets after meals. Gives a loud call that sounds like a machine gun. Mates know each other by their calls. Digs a tunnel up to 4 feet (1 m) long to a nest chamber. Small white patches on dark wing tips flash during flight.

Chestnut-backed Chickadee
Poecile rufescens

YEAR-ROUND

Size: 4¾" (12 cm)

Male: Rich, warm chestnut back and sides. Black crown and chin. White cheeks and sides of head. Gray wings and tail.

Female: same as male

Juvenile: same as adult

Nest: cavity; female and male build; 1–2 broods per year

Eggs: 5–7; white without markings

Incubation: 10–12 days; female incubates

Fledging: 13–16 days; female and male feed the young

Migration: non-migrator

When Seen: year-round

Food: insects, seeds, fruit; comes to seed and suet feeders

Compare: Black-capped Chickadee (p. 221) and Mountain Chickadee (p. 223) lack Chestnut-backed's distinctive chestnut back.

Stan's Notes: The most colorful of all chickadees. Like the other chickadee species, the Chestnut-backed clings to branches upside down, looking for insects. During breeding, it is quiet and secretive. In winter it joins other birds such as kinglets, woodpeckers and other chickadees. Prefers humid coastal coniferous forests with hemlock and Tamarack. Builds a cavity nest 2–20 feet (up to 6 m) above the ground. Will use the same nest year after year. In late summer, some move to higher elevations and back down just before winter starts. Can be attracted to your yard with nest boxes. Comes to seed and suet feeders.

Brown Creeper
Certhia americana

Size: 5" (13 cm)

Male: Small, thin, nearly camouflaged brown bird. White from chin to belly. White eyebrows. Dark eyes and a thin, curved bill. Tail is long and stiff.

Female: same as male

Juvenile: same as adults

Nest: cup; female constructs; 1 brood per year

Eggs: 5–6; white with tiny brown markings

Incubation: 14–17 days; female incubates; male feeds the female during incubation

Fledging: 13–16 days; female and male feed the young

Migration: partial migrator to non-migrator; moves around to find food in winter

Food: insects, nuts, seeds

Compare: The Red-breasted Nuthatch (p. 217) and White-breasted Nuthatch (p. 227) climb down tree trunks, not up. To spot a Brown Creeper, look for a small brown bird with a white belly creeping up trees.

Stan's Notes: A forest bird, commonly found in wooded habitats. Will fly from the top of one tree trunk to the bottom of another, then work its way to the top, looking for caterpillars, spider eggs and more. Its long tail has tiny spines underneath, which help it cling to trees. Uses its camouflage coloring to hide in plain sight: it spreads out flat on a branch or trunk and won't move. Often builds its nest behind the loose bark of a dead or dying tree. Young follow their parents around, creeping up trees soon after fledging.

Chipping Sparrow
Spizella passerina

SUMMER

Size: 5" (13 cm)

Male: Small gray-brown sparrow with clear-gray chest. Rusty crown. White eyebrows and thin black eye line. Thin gray-black bill. Two faint wing bars.

Female: same as male

Juvenile: similar to adults, with streaking on the chest; lacks a rusty crown

Nest: cup; female builds; 2 broods per year

Eggs: 3–5; blue-green with brown markings

Incubation: 11–14 days; female incubates

Fledging: 10–12 days; female and male feed the young

Migration: complete, to southwestern states, Mexico and Central America

Food: insects, seeds; will come to ground feeders

Compare: The Fox Sparrow (p. 129) is larger and lacks the rusty crown. Song Sparrow (p. 105) and female House Finch (p. 101) have heavily streaked chests. Look for the rusty crown and black eye line to help identify the Chipping Sparrow.

Stan's Notes: A common garden or yard bird, often seen feeding on dropped seeds beneath feeders. Gathers in large family groups to feed in preparation for migration. Migrates at night in flocks of 20–30 birds. The common name comes from the male's fast "chip" call. Often is just called Chippy. Builds nest low in dense shrubs and almost always lines it with animal hair. Comfortable with people, allowing you to approach closely before it flies away.

Pine Siskin
Spinus pinus

Size: 5" (13 cm)

Male: Small brown finch with heavy streaking on the back, breast and belly. Yellow wing bars. Yellow at the base of tail. Thin bill.

Female: similar to male, with less yellow

Juvenile: similar to adult, with a light-yellow tinge over the breast and chin

Nest: cup; female builds; 2 broods

Eggs: 3–4; greenish blue with brown markings

Incubation: 12–13 days; female incubates

Fledging: 14–15 days; female and male feed the young

Migration: non-migrator to irruptive; moves around the U.S. in search of food in some winters

Food: seeds, insects; will come to seed feeders

Compare: Female House Finch (p. 101) lacks any yellow. The female American Goldfinch (p. 325) has white wing bars. Female Purple Finch (p. 117) has bold white eyebrows. Look for the yellow wing bars to identify the Pine Siskin.

Stan's Notes: A nesting resident in coniferous forests. Nests mostly in the western half of Washington, with nests only a few feet apart. Builds nest toward the end of coniferous branches, where needles are dense, helping to conceal. Will come to thistle feeders. Gives a series of high-pitched, wheezy calls. Also gives a wheezing twitter. Breeds in small groups. Male feeds the female during incubation. Juveniles lose the yellow tint by late summer of their first year. Gathers in flocks in autumn, moves around Washington and visits bird feeders.

male
p. 297

female

House Finch
Haemorhous mexicanus

Size: 5" (13 cm)

YEAR-ROUND

Female: Plain brown with heavy streaking on a white chest.

Male: red-to-orange face, throat, chest and rump; streaked belly and wings; brown cap; brown marking behind the eyes

Juvenile: similar to female

Nest: cup, occasionally in a cavity; female builds; 2 broods per year

Eggs: 4–5; pale blue, lightly marked

Incubation: 12–14 days; female incubates

Fledging: 15–19 days; female and male feed the young

Migration: non-migrator to partial migrator; will move around to find food

Food: seeds, fruit, leaf buds; visits seed feeders and feeders that offer grape jelly

Compare: Female Cassin's Finch (p. 123) has a more heavily streaked belly. Pine Siskin (p. 99) is similar but has yellow wing bars and a smaller bill. Very similar female Purple Finch (p. 117) has bold white eyebrows.

Stan's Notes: Can be a common bird at your feeders. A very social bird, visiting feeders in small flocks. Likes to nest in hanging flower baskets. Male sings a loud, cheerful warbling song. Historically it occurred from the Pacific Coast to the Rockies, with only a few reaching the eastern side. House Finches that were originally introduced to Long Island, New York, from the western U.S. in the 1940s have since populated the entire eastern U.S. Suffers from a disease that causes the eyes to crust, resulting in blindness and death.

House Wren

Troglodytes aedon

SUMMER

Size: 5" (13 cm)

Male: All-brown bird with lighter-brown markings on the wings and tail. Slightly curved brown bill. Often holds tail upward.

Female: same as male

Juvenile: same as adult

Nest: cavity; female and male line just about any nest cavity; 2 broods per year

Eggs: 4–6; tan with brown markings

Incubation: 10–13 days; female and male incubate

Fledging: 12–15 days; female and male feed the young

Migration: complete, to southern states and Mexico

Food: insects, spiders, snails

Compare: Bewick's Wren (p. 107) has white eyebrows and white spots on the tail. House Wren's lack of eyebrows distinguishes it from other wrens. Look for House Wren's long curved bill and long upturned tail to differentiate it from sparrows.

Stan's Notes: A prolific songster. During the mating season, sings from dawn to dusk. Seen in brushy yards, parks and woodlands and along forest edges. Easily attracted to a nest box. In spring, the male chooses several prospective nesting cavities and places a few small twigs in each. The female inspects all of them and finishes constructing the nest in the cavity of her choice. She fills the cavity with short twigs and then lines a small depression at the back with pine needles and grass. She often has trouble fitting longer twigs through the entrance hole and tries many different directions and approaches until she is successful.

103

Song Sparrow
Melospiza melodia

YEAR-ROUND

Size: 5–6" (13–15 cm)

Male: Common brown sparrow with heavy dark streaks on the chest coalescing into a central dark spot.

Female: same as male

Juvenile: similar to adults, with a finely streaked chest; lacks a central dark spot

Nest: cup; female builds; 2 broods per year

Eggs: 3–4; blue to green, with red-brown markings

Incubation: 12–14 days; female incubates

Fledging: 9–12 days; female and male feed the young

Migration: non-migrator; moves around to find food in winter

Food: insects, seeds; only rarely comes to ground feeders with seeds

Compare: Similar to other brown sparrows. Look for the heavily streaked chest with a central dark spot to help identify the Song Sparrow.

Stan's Notes: There are many subspecies of this bird, but the dark spot in the center of the chest appears in every variety. A constant songster, repeating its loud, clear song every few minutes. The song varies from region to region but has the same basic structure. Sings from thick shrubs to defend a small territory, beginning with three notes and finishing up with a trill. A ground feeder, it will "double-scratch" with both feet at the same time to expose seeds. When the female builds a new nest for a second brood, the male often takes over feeding the first brood. Unlike many other sparrow species, Song Sparrows rarely flock together. A common host of the Brown-headed Cowbird.

Bewick's Wren
Thryomanes bewickii

YEAR-ROUND WINTER

Size: 5½" (14 cm)

Male: Brown cap, back, wings and tail. Gray chest and belly. White chin and eyebrows. Long tail with white spots on edges is cocked and flits sideways. Pointed down-curved bill.

Female: same as male

Juvenile: similar to adult

Nest: cavity; female and male build nest in woodpecker hole or nest box; 2–3 broods a year

Eggs: 4–8; white with brown markings

Incubation: 12–14 days; female incubates

Fledging: 10–14 days; female and male feed the young

Migration: non-migrator to partial migrator; will move around to find food in winter

Food: insects, seeds

Compare: The House Wren (p. 103) is slightly smaller and lacks the obvious white eyebrow marks and white spots on tail.

Stan's Notes: A common wren of backyards and gardens. Insects make up 97 percent of its diet, with plant seeds composing the rest. Competes with House Wrens for nesting cavities. Male will choose nesting cavities and start to build nests using small uniform-sized sticks. Female will make the final selection of a nest site and finish building. Begins breeding in April. Has 2–3 broods per year. Male feeds female while she incubates. Average size territory per pair is 5 acres (2 ha), which they defend all year long. Birds that breed in higher elevations retreat to lower elevations for the winter. Has been expanding its range in eastern Washington.

male
p. 225

female

Oregon
female

Dark-eyed Junco

Junco hyemalis

YEAR-ROUND
WINTER

Size: 5½" (14 cm)

Female: A plump, dark-eyed bird with a tan-to-brown chest, head and back. White belly. Ivory-to-pink bill. White outer tail feathers appear like a white V in flight.

Male: round bird with gray plumage

Juvenile: similar to female, with streaking on the breast and head

Nest: cup; female and male build; 2 broods per year

Eggs: 3–5; white with reddish-brown markings

Incubation: 12–13 days; female incubates

Fledging: 10–13 days; male and female feed the young

Migration: non migrator to partial migrator

Food: seeds, insects; visits ground and seed feeders

Compare: Rarely confused with any other bird. Look for the ivory-to-pink bill and small flocks feeding beneath seed feeders to help identify the female Dark-eyed Junco.

Stan's Notes: A common year-round resident. One of the most numerous wintering birds in the state, spending winters in foothills and plains after snowmelt, returning to higher elevations for nesting. Adheres to a rigid social hierarchy, with dominant birds chasing the less dominant birds. Look for the white outer tail feathers flashing in flight. Often seen in small flocks on the ground, where it uses its feet to simultaneously "double-scratch" to expose seeds and insects. Eats many weed seeds. Nests in a wide variety of wooded habitats in April and May. Several subspecies of Dark-eyed Junco were previously considered to be separate species (see lower inset).

female

male
p. 77

Lazuli Bunting
Passerina amoena

SUMMER

Size: 5½" (14 cm)

Female: Overall grayish brown with a warm brown chest, light wash of blue on wings and tail, gray throat and light-gray belly. Two narrow white wing bars.

Male: turquoise-blue head, neck, back and tail, cinnamon breast, white belly, 2 bold white wing bars

Juvenile: similar to adult of the same sex

Nest: cup; female builds; 2–3 broods per year

Eggs: 3–5; pale blue without markings

Incubation: 11–13 days; female incubates

Fledging: 10–12 days; female and male feed the young

Migration: complete, to Mexico

Food: insects, seeds

Compare: The female Western (p. 85) and Mountain (p. 83) Bluebirds are larger and have much more blue than female Bunting.

Stan's Notes: More common in low-elevation shrublands in the eastern portion of the state; less common in western Washington. Doesn't like dense forests. Strong association with water such as rivers and streams. Gathers in small flocks and tends to move up in elevations after breeding to hunt for insects and look for seeds. Has increased in population and expanded its range over the last century. Males sing from short shrubs and scrubby areas to attract females. Rarely perches on tall trees. Each male has his own unique combination of notes to produce his "own" song. Young males often copy songs of older males in the area.

Cliff Swallow
Petrochelidon pyrrhonota

SUMMER

Size: 5½" (14 cm)

Male: Uniquely patterned swallow with a dark back, wings and cap. Distinctive tan-to-rust rump, cheeks and forehead.

Female: same as male

Juvenile: similar to adult, lacks distinct patterning

Nest: gourd-shaped, made of mud; male and female build; 1–2 broods per year

Eggs: 4–6; pale white with brown markings

Incubation: 14–16 days; male and female incubate

Fledging: 21–24 days; female and male feed young

Migration: complete, to South America

Food: insects

Compare: Barn Swallow (p. 81) is larger and has a distinctive, deeply forked tail and blue back and wings. Tree Swallow (p. 79) lacks any tan-to-rust coloring. Violet-green Swallow (p. 277) is green with a bright-white face.

Stan's Notes: A common and widespread species in Washington. Common around bridges (especially bridges over water) and rural housing (especially in open country near cliffs). Builds a gourd-shaped nest with a funnel-like entrance pointing down. A colony nester, with many nests lined up beneath building eaves or cliff overhangs. Will carry balls of mud up to a mile to construct its nest. Many in the colony return to the same nest site each year. Not unusual to have two broods per season. If the number of nests underneath eaves becomes a problem, wait until the young have left the nests to hose off the mud.

House Sparrow
Passer domesticus

YEAR-ROUND

Size: 6" (15 cm)

Male: Brown back with a gray belly and cap. Large black patch extending from the throat to the chest (bib). One white wing bar.

Female: slightly smaller than the male; light brown with light eyebrows; lacks a bib and white wing bar

Juvenile: similar to female

Nest: cavity; female and male build a domed cup nest within; 2–3 broods per year

Eggs: 4–6; white with brown markings

Incubation: 10–12 days; female incubates

Fledging: 14–17 days; female and male feed the young

Migration: non-migrator; moves around to find food

Food: seeds, insects, fruit; comes to seed feeders

Compare: Chipping Sparrow (p. 97) has a rusty crown. Look for the black bib to identify the male House Sparrow and the clear breast to help identify the female.

Stan's Notes: One of the first birdsongs heard in cities in spring. A familiar city bird, nearly always in small flocks. Also found on farms. Introduced in 1850 from Europe to Central Park in New York. Now seen throughout North America. Related to old-world sparrows; not a relative of any sparrows in the U.S. An aggressive bird that will kill young birds in order to take over the nest cavity. Uses dried grass and small scraps of plastic, paper and other materials to build an oversize, domed nest in the cavity.

male
p. 299

female

Purple Finch

Haemorhous purpureus

YEAR-ROUND

Size: 6" (15 cm)

Female: Plain brown with heavy streaking on the chest. Bold white eyebrows and a large bill.

Male: raspberry-red head, cap, breast, back and rump; brownish wings and tail

Juvenile: same as female

Nest: cup; female and male build; 1 brood per year

Eggs: 4–5; greenish blue with brown markings

Incubation: 12–13 days; female incubates

Fledging: 13–14 days; female and male feed the young

Migration: non-migrator to irruptive; moves around in search of food

Food: seeds, insects, fruit; comes to seed feeders

Compare: The female House Finch (p. 101) lacks eyebrows. Pine Siskin (p. 99) has yellow wing bars and a much smaller bill than the Purple Finch. The female American Goldfinch (p. 325) has a clear chest. Look for the bold white eyebrows to identify the female Purple Finch.

Stan's Notes: A year-round resident, common in non-residential areas. Prefers open woods or woodland edges of low to middle elevation conifer forest. Feeds mainly on seeds; ash tree seeds are an important source of food. Travels in flocks of up to 50 birds. Visits seed feeders along with House Finches, which makes it hard to tell them apart. Flies in the typical undulating, up-and-down pattern of finches. Sings a rich, loud song. Gives a distinctive "tic" note only in flight. The male is not purple. The Latin species name *purpureus* means "purple" (and other reddish colors).

male

female

Gray-crowned Rosy-Finch
Leucosticte tephrocotis

YEAR-ROUND
WINTER

Size: 6" (15 cm)

Male: Gray crown with a black forehead, chin and throat. Warm cinnamon-brown body with a wash of rosy red, especially along flanks and rump.

Female: same as male, but has less red

Juvenile: similar to adult of the same sex

Nest: cup; female builds; 1–2 broods per year

Eggs: 3–5; white without markings

Incubation: 12–14 days; female incubates

Fledging: 16–18 days; female and male feed young

Migration: non-migrator to partial; moves around in winter

Food: seeds, insects; will visit seed feeders

Compare: Similar to other rosy-finches, but the Gray-crowned has a black forehead, throat and chin. The female Cassin's Finch (p. 123) and female House Finch (p. 101) lack the characteristic gray crown of the Gray-crowned Rosy-Finch.

Stan's Notes: Found in high alpine regions, nesting in steep cliff faces. Year-round resident, but breeding birds in Canada and Alaska move into the state during winter, swelling the population. Breeds in the Rocky Mountains of Canada and the U.S. Almost always seen in small flocks, foraging on the ground near patches of snow in high elevations. During breeding, both male and female develop an opening in the floor of the mouth (buccal pouch), which is used to carry a large supply of food, such as insects, to young in the nest.

white-striped

tan-striped

White-throated Sparrow
Zonotrichia albicollis

MIGRATION
WINTER

Size: 6–7" (15–18 cm)

Male: Brown with a gray or tan chest and belly. White or tan throat patch and eyebrows. Bold striping on the head. Small yellow spot by each eye (lore).

Female: same as male

Juvenile: similar to adult, with a heavily streaked chest and gray throat and eyebrows

Nest: cup; female builds; 1 brood per year

Eggs: 4–6; green-to-blue or cream-white with red-brown markings

Incubation: 11–14 days; female incubates

Fledging: 10–12 days; female and male feed the young

Migration: complete migrator, to Washington and southwestern states

Food: insects, seeds, fruit; visits ground feeders

Compare: White-crowned Sparrow (p. 125) lacks the throat patch and yellow lores of the White-throated Sparrow.

Stan's Notes: Two color variations (polymorphic): white-striped and tan-striped. Studies indicate that the white-striped adults tend to mate with the tan-striped birds. It's not clear why. Known for its wonderful song. Sings all year and can even be heard at night. White- and tan-striped males and white-striped females sing, but tan-striped females do not. Builds nest on the ground under small trees in bogs and coniferous forests. Often associated with other sparrows in winter. Feeds on the ground under feeders. Immature and first-year females tend to winter farther south than the adults.

male
p. 301

female

Cassin's Finch
Haemorhous cassinii

YEAR-ROUND
SUMMER

Size: 6½" (16 cm)

Female: Brown-to-gray finch with fine black streaks on back and wings. Heavily streaked white chest and belly.

Male: light wash of crimson red, especially bright red crown, brown streaks on the back and wings, white belly

Juvenile: similar to female

Nest: cup; female builds; 1–2 broods per year

Eggs: 3–5; white without markings

Incubation: 12–14 days; female incubates

Fledging: 14–18 days; female and male feed young

Migration: partial migrator to non-migrator; will move around to find food

Food: seeds, insects, fruits, berries; will visit seed feeders

Compare: The female House Finch (p. 101) is similar, but it has a gray belly that is not as streaked. Lacks the characteristic gray head markings of the Gray-crowned Rosy-Finch (p. 119).

Stan's Notes: This is a mountain finch of eastern Washington's coniferous forests. Usually forages for seeds on the ground, but it also eats evergreen buds and aspen and willow catkins. Breeds in May. A colony nester, depending on the regional source of food. The more food available, the larger the colony. Male sings a rapid warble, often imitating other birds such as jays, tanagers and grosbeaks. A cowbird host.

juvenile

White-crowned Sparrow

Zonotrichia leucophrys

YEAR-ROUND
WINTER

Size: 6½–7½" (16.5–19 cm)

Male: Brown with a gray chest and black-and-white striped crown. Small, thin, pink bill.

Female: same as male

Juvenile: similar to adults, with black and brown stripes on the head

Nest: cup; female builds; 2 broods per year

Eggs: 3–5; greenish to bluish to whitish with red-brown markings

Incubation: 11–14 days; female incubates

Fledging: 8–12 days; male and female feed the young

Migration: complete, to western coastal U.S., southern states and Mexico; non-migrator in parts of Washington

Food: insects, seeds, berries; visits ground feeders

Compare: Golden-crowned Sparrow (p. 127) has a central yellow spot on the crown. Look for the striped crown to help identify the White-crowned Sparrow.

Stan's Notes: Year-round resident in parts of the state. Often in groups of up to 20 birds during winter, when it can be seen visiting ground feeders and feeding beneath seed feeders. This ground feeder will "double-scratch" backward with both feet simultaneously to find seeds. Prefers scrubby areas, woodland edges, and open or grassy habitats. The males are prolific songsters, singing in late winter while migrating north. Males take most of the responsibility for raising the young while females start their second broods. Only 9–12 days separate the broods.

juvenile

winter

Golden-crowned Sparrow
Zonotrichia atricapilla

MIGRATION
WINTER

Size: 7" (18 cm)

Male: All-brown sparrow with a heavy body, long tail and yellow spot in the center of a black crown. Gray around head and chest. Upper bill (mandible) is darker than the lower bill (mandible). Winter has varying amounts of black on crown.

Female: same as male

Juvenile: similar to adult, lacks the black and yellow crown

Nest: cup; female and male build; 1 brood a year

Eggs: 3–5; bluish white with brown markings

Incubation: 10–14 days; female incubates

Fledging: 8–14 days; male and female feed the young

Migration: complete, to western coastal U.S., Mexico

Food: insects, seeds, berries

Compare: The White-crowned Sparrow (p. 125) is similar, but it lacks the yellow patch in the center of Golden-crowned's black crown.

Stan's Notes: One of the common winter sparrows, often seen in flocks with other sparrows. In the winter there are varying amounts of black on the head, but the yellow patch remains the same. Male feeds the female while she incubates. Nests in western Canada and Alaska, not in Washington. Found in weedy or shrubby areas, along forest edges. A ground feeder often seen scratching the ground under seed and suet feeders. Also feeds on dried and fresh fruits, flower buds and insects.

Slate-colored

Pacific
sooty

Fox Sparrow
Passerella iliaca

SUMMER
WINTER

Size: 7" (18 cm)

Male: A plump, brown sparrow with a gray head, back and rump. White chest and belly with rusty brown streaks. Rusty tail and wings.

Female: same as male

Juvenile: same as adult

Nest: cup; female builds; 2 broods per year

Eggs: 2–4; pale green with reddish markings

Incubation: 12–14 days; female incubates

Fledging: 10–11 days; male and female feed the young

Migration: complete, to western coastal U.S. and southern states

Food: seeds, insects; comes to ground feeders

Compare: The Spotted Towhee (p. 29) is found in similar habitats, but the male towhee has a black head and both male and female have white bellies.

Stan's Notes: One of the largest sparrows. Often alone or in small groups. Found in shrubby areas, open fields and backyards. Comes to ground feeders and seen underneath seed feeders during migration, searching for seeds and insects. The winter Fox Sparrows are not the same variety as the resident summer breeders. In winter, northern Pacific varieties (shown), which are a dark brown, displace breeding Slate-colored Fox Sparrows (see inset), which have gray heads and backs. Nests in brush on the ground and along forest edges. Scratches like a chicken with both feet at the same time to find seeds and insects. The name "Sparrow" comes from the Anglo-Saxon word *spearwa*, meaning "flutterer," as applies to any small bird. "Fox" refers to the bird's rusty color.

129

Swainson's Thrush

Catharus ustulatus

SUMMER

Size: 7" (18 cm)

Male: Dusty-brown head, back and wings. Brown smudges and spots, especially beneath chin, on the chest and on an off-white belly. Small, thin two-toned bill, yellow under and black above.

Female: same as male

Juvenile: similar to adult, less distinct spots on chest

Nest: cup; female builds; 1 brood per year

Eggs: 3–5; pale blue with brown markings

Incubation: 12–14 days; female incubates

Fledging: 10–14 days; female and male feed young

Migration: complete, to Mexico, Central America and South America

Food: insects, fruit

Compare: American Robin (p. 245) is similar in shape, but it is larger and has a red breast and a gray head and back.

Stan's Notes: The most common of the thrush species in the state. Found throughout western Washington in lower-elevation conifer forests. Often hard to see because most of the time it stays on the ground in thick vegetation. Feeds mostly on insects in spring and summer, adding fruit to its diet in late summer. Nests in shrubs or low in conifer trees, building a bulky cup nest consisting of grass, bark and moss, all glued together with mud.

131

female

male

Horned Lark
Eremophila alpestris

YEAR-ROUND WINTER

Size: 7–8" (18–20 cm)

Male: Tan to brown with black markings on the face. Black necklace and bill. Pale-yellow chin. Two tiny feather "horns" on the top of the head, sometimes hard to see. Dark tail with white outer tail feathers, seen in flight.

Female: duller than male; less noticeable "horns"

Juvenile: lacks a yellow chin and black markings; does not develop "horns" until the second year

Nest: ground; female builds; 2–3 broods per year

Eggs: 3–4; gray with brown markings

Incubation: 11–12 days; female incubates

Fledging: 9–12 days; female and male feed the young

Migration: partial migrator to non-migrator, to coastal Washington, southern states, Mexico, Central and South America

Food: seeds, insects

Compare: Western Meadowlark (p. 343) is larger and has a yellow breast and belly. Look for the black markings by the eyes and the black necklace to identify the Horned Lark.

Stan's Notes: The only true lark native to North America. A bird of open ground. Common in rural areas; often seen in large flocks. The population increased in North America over the past century as more land was cleared for farming. Male performs a fluttering courtship flight high in the air while singing a high-pitched song. Female performs a fluttering distraction display when the nest is disturbed. Moves around in winter to find food. "Lark" comes from the Middle English *laverock*, or "a lark."

male
p. 25

female

Brown-headed Cowbird

Molothrus ater

YEAR-ROUND
SUMMER

Size: 7½" (19 cm)

Female: Dull brown with no obvious markings. Pointed, sharp, gray bill. Dark eyes.

Male: glossy black with a chocolate-brown head

Juvenile: similar to female but with dull-gray plumage and a streaked chest

Nest: no nest; lays eggs in the nests of other birds

Eggs: 5–7; white with brown markings

Incubation: 10–13 days; host bird incubates the eggs

Fledging: 10–11 days; host birds feed the young

Migration: complete, to southern states; non-migrator in parts of Washington

Food: insects, seeds; will come to seed feeders

Compare: The female Red-winged Blackbird (p. 145) has white eyebrows and heavy streaking. European Starling (p. 27) has speckles and a shorter tail. The pointed gray bill helps to identify the female Brown-headed Cowbird.

Stan's Notes: Cowbirds are members of the blackbird family. Of approximately 750 species of parasitic birds worldwide, this is the only parasitic bird in Washington. Brood parasites lay their eggs in the nests of other birds, leaving the host birds to raise their young. Cowbirds are known to have laid their eggs in the nests of over 200 species of birds. While some birds reject cowbird eggs, most incubate them and raise the young, even to the exclusion of their own. Look for warblers and other birds feeding young birds twice their own size. Named "Cowbird" for its habit of following bison and cattle herds to feed on insects flushed up by the animals.

1 year
old

Bohemian
Waxwing

Cedar Waxwing
Bombycilla cedrorum

YEAR-ROUND

Size: 7½" (19 cm)

Male: Sleek-looking, gray-to-brown bird. Pointed crest, bandit-like mask and light-yellow belly. Bold-yellow tip of tail. Red wing tips look like they were dipped in red wax.

Female: same as male

Juvenile: grayish with a heavily streaked breast; lacks the sleek look, black mask and red wing tips

Nest: cup; female and male construct; 1 brood per year, occasionally 2

Eggs: 4–6; pale blue with brown markings

Incubation: 10–12 days; female incubates

Fledging: 14–18 days; female and male feed the young

Migration: non-migrator; moves around to find food

Food: cedar cones, fruit, insects

Compare: Similar to its larger, less common cousin, Bohemian Waxwing. Look for the red wing tips, yellow-tipped tail and black mask to identify the Cedar Waxwing.

Stan's Notes: The name is derived from its red, wax-like wing tips and preference for the small, berry-like cones of the cedar. Seen in flocks, moving around from area to area looking for berries. Feeds on insects during summer, before berries are abundant. Wanders during winter, searching for food supplies. Spends most of its time at the top of tall trees. Listen for the high-pitched "sreee" whistling sound it constantly makes while perched or in flight. Obtains the mask after the first year and red wing tips after the second year.

male
p. 293

female

SUMMER

Black-headed Grosbeak
Pheucticus melanocephalus

Size: 8" (20 cm)

Female: Appears like an overgrown sparrow. Overall brown with a lighter breast and belly. Large two-toned bill. Prominent white eyebrows. Yellow wing linings, as seen in flight.

Male: burnt-orange chest, neck and rump, black head, tail and wings with irregular-shaped white wing patches, large bill with upper bill darker than lower

Juvenile: similar to adult of the same sex

Nest: cup; female builds; 1 brood per year

Eggs: 3–4; pale green or bluish, brown markings

Incubation: 11–13 days; female and male incubate

Fledging: 11–13 days; female and male feed young

Migration: complete, to Mexico, Central America and South America

Food: seeds, insects, fruit; comes to seed feeders

Compare: Female House Finch (p. 101) is smaller, has more streaking on the chest and the bill isn't as large. Look for female Grosbeak's unusual bicolored bill.

Stan's Notes: A cosmopolitan bird that nests in a wide variety of habitats, seeming to prefer the foothills more than other places. Both the male and female sing and will aggressively defend the nest against intruders. Song is very similar to American Robin's (p. 245) and Western Tanager (p. 335), making it hard to tell them apart by song. Populations increasing in Washington and across the U.S.

winter

breeding

Spotted Sandpiper
Actitis macularius

YEAR-ROUND
SUMMER

Size: 8" (20 cm)

Male: Olive-brown back with black spots on a white chest and belly. White line over eyes. Long, dull-yellow legs. Long bill. Winter plumage lacks spots on the chest and belly.

Female: same as male

Juvenile: similar to winter plumage, with a darker bill

Nest: ground; male builds; 2 broods per year

Eggs: 3–4; brownish with brown markings

Incubation: 20–24 days; male incubates

Fledging: 17–21 days; male feeds the young

Migration: complete, to southern states, Mexico, Central and South America; non-migrator in coastal Washington

Food: aquatic insects

Compare: Killdeer (p. 155) has 2 black neck bands. Look for the black spots on the chest and belly and the bobbing tail to help identify the breeding Spotted Sandpiper.

Stan's Notes: Seen along the shorelines of large ponds, lakes and rivers. One of the few shorebirds that will dive underwater when pursued. Able to fly straight up out of the water. Holds wings in a cup-like arc in flight, rarely lifting them above a horizontal plane. Walks as if delicately balanced. When standing, constantly bobs its tail. Gives a rapid series of "weet-weet-weet" calls when frightened and flying away. Female mates with multiple males and lays eggs in up to five nests. Male does all of the nest building, incubating and childcare without any help from the female.

breeding

winter
p. 239

Dunlin
Calidris alpina

MIGRATION
WINTER

Size: 8–9" (20–23 cm)

Male: Breeding adult is distinctive with a rusty-red back, finely streaked chest and an obvious black patch on the belly. Stout bill, curving slightly downward at the tip. Black legs.

Female: slightly larger than male, with a longer bill

Juvenile: slightly rusty back with a spotty chest

Nest: ground; male and female construct; 1 brood per year

Eggs: 2–4; olive-buff or blue-green with red-brown markings

Incubation: 21–22 days; male incubates during the day, female incubates at night

Fledging: 19–21 days; male feeds the young, female often leaves before the young fledge

Migration: complete, to the coasts of the U.S., Mexico and Central America

Food: insects

Compare: A unique shorebird. Look for the obvious black belly patch and down-curved bill of breeding Dunlin.

Stan's Notes: Breeding plumage more commonly seen in spring. Flights include heights of up to 100 feet (30 m) with brief gliding alternating with shallow flutters, and a rhythmic, repeating song. Huge flocks fly synchronously, with birds twisting and turning, flashing light and dark undersides. Males tend to fly farther south in winter than females. Doesn't nest in the state.

male
p. 31

female

Red-winged Blackbird
Agelaius phoeniceus

YEAR-ROUND

Size: 8½" (22 cm)

Female: Heavily streaked brown body. Pointed brown bill and white eyebrows.

Male: jet black with red-and-yellow shoulder patches (epaulets) and a pointed black bill

Juvenile: same as female

Nest: cup; female builds; 2–3 broods per year

Eggs: 3–4; bluish green with brown markings

Incubation: 10–12 days; female incubates

Fledging: 11–14 days; female and male feed the young

Migration: non-migrator to partial migrator; moves around in winter to find food

Food: seeds, insects; visits seed and suet feeders

Compare: Female Brown-headed Cowbird (p. 135) is smaller. Female Brewer's Blackbird (p. 147) and Yellow-headed Blackbird (p. 151) are larger. All three species lack white eyebrows and streaks on chest. Look for white eyebrows and heavy streaking to identify the female Red-winged Blackbird.

Stan's Notes: One of the most widespread and numerous birds in the state. Found around marshes, wetlands, lakes and rivers. Flocks with as many as 10,000 birds have been reported. Males arrive before females and sing to defend their territory. The male repeats his call from the top of a cattail while showing off his red-and-yellow shoulder patches. The female chooses a mate and often builds her nest over shallow water in a thick stand of cattails. The male can be aggressive when defending the nest. Feeds mostly on seeds in spring and fall, and insects throughout the summer.

male
p. 33

female

Brewer's Blackbird
Euphagus cyanocephalus

YEAR-ROUND
WINTER

Size: 9" (22.5 cm)

Female: Overall grayish brown. Legs and bill nearly black. While most have dark eyes, some have bright-white or pale-yellow eyes.

Male: glossy black, shining green in direct light, head purplish, white or pale-yellow eyes

Juvenile: similar to female

Nest: cup; female builds; 1–2 broods per year

Eggs: 4–6; gray with brown markings

Incubation: 12–14 days; female incubates

Fledging: 13–14 days; female and male feed young

Migration: non-migrator to partial migrator

Food: insects, seeds, fruit

Compare: Female Brown-headed Cowbird (p. 135) is smaller and lighter in color. Female Red-winged Blackbird (p. 145) is similar in size, but it has a heavily streaked chest and prominent white eyebrows.

Stan's Notes: Common blackbird of open areas such as farms, wet pastures, mountain meadows and even desert scrub. Male and some females are easily identified by their bright, nearly white eyes. It is a common cowbird host, usually nesting in a shrub, small tree or directly on the ground. Prefers to nest in small colonies of up to 20 pairs. Gathers in large flocks with cowbirds, Red-wingeds and other blackbirds to migrate. It is expanding its range in North America.

female

male

Common Nighthawk
Chordeiles minor

SUMMER

Size: 9" (23 cm)

Male: Camouflaged brown and white with a white chin. Distinctive white band across the wings and tail, seen only in flight.

Female: similar to male, with a tan chin; lacks a white tail band

Juvenile: similar to female

Nest: no nest; lays eggs on the ground, usually on rocks, or on rooftop; 1 brood per year

Eggs: 2; cream with lavender markings

Incubation: 19–20 days; female and male incubate

Fledging: 20–21 days; female and male feed the young

Migration: complete, to South America

Food: insects caught in the air

Compare: Look for the white chin, obvious white band on the wings and characteristic flap-flap-flap-glide pattern to help identify the Common Nighthawk.

Stan's Notes: Usually only seen in flight at dusk or after sunset but not uncommon to see it sleeping on a branch during the day. A prolific insect eater and very noisy in flight, repeating a "peenting" call. Alternates slow wingbeats with bursts of quick wingbeats. In cities, prefers to nest on flat rooftops with gravel. City populations are on the decline as gravel rooftops are converted to other styles. In spring, the male performs a showy mating ritual consisting of a steep diving flight ending with a loud popping noise. One of the first birds to migrate each fall. Often seen in large flocks.

male
p. 35

female

Yellow-headed Blackbird
Xanthocephalus xanthocephalus

SUMMER

Size:	9–11" (23–28 cm)
Female:	Large brown bird with a dull-yellow head and chest. Slightly smaller than the male.
Male:	black bird with a lemon-yellow head, breast and nape of neck, black mask, gray bill and white wing patches
Juvenile:	similar to female
Nest:	cup; female builds; 2 broods per year
Eggs:	3–5; greenish white with brown markings
Incubation:	11–13 days; female incubates
Fledging:	9–12 days; female feeds the young
Migration:	complete, to southern states and Mexico
Food:	insects, seeds; will come to ground feeders
Compare:	Female Red-winged Blackbird (p. 145) is smaller and has white eyebrows and heavy streaking. Look for the dull-yellow head to help identify the female Yellow-headed.

Stan's Notes: Found around marshes, wetland and lakes. Nests in deep water, unlike its cousin, the Red-winged Blackbird, which prefers shallow water. Usually heard before seen. Gives a raspy, low, metallic-sounding call. The male is the only large black bird with a bright-yellow head. He gives an impressive mating display, flying with his head drooped and feet and tail pointing down while steadily beating his wings. Young keep low and out of sight for up to three weeks before they start to fly. Migrates in large flocks of as many as 200 birds, often with Red-winged Blackbirds and Brown-headed Cowbirds. Flocks of mainly males return in late March and early April; females return later. Most colonies consist of 20–100 nests.

151

in flight

juvenile

male

female

in-flight
juvenile

American Kestrel
Falco sparverius

YEAR-ROUND
WINTER

Size: 9–11" (23–28 cm); up to 2' wingspan

Male: Rust-brown back and tail. White breast with dark spots. Two vertical black lines on a white face. Blue-gray wings. Wide black band with a white edge on the tip of a rusty tail.

Female: similar to male but slightly larger, with rust-brown wings and dark bands on the tail

Juvenile: same as adult of the same sex

Nest: cavity; does not build a nest; 1 brood per year

Eggs: 4–5; white with brown markings

Incubation: 29–31 days; male and female incubate

Fledging: 30–31 days; female and male feed the young

Migration: non-migrator to partial migrator

Food: insects, small mammals and birds, reptiles

Compare: The Peregrine Falcon (p. 261) is much larger and has a dark "hood" marking. Look for the two vertical stripes on the face of the Kestrel. No other small bird of prey has a rusty back and tail.

Stan's Notes: An unusual raptor because the sexes look different (dimorphic). Due to its small size, this falcon was once called a Sparrow Hawk. Hovers near roads, then dives for prey. Watch for it to pump its tail after landing on a perch. Perches nearly upright. Eats many grasshoppers. Adapts quickly to a wooden nest box. Can be extremely vocal, giving a loud series of high-pitched calls. Ability to see ultraviolet (UV) light helps it locate mice and other prey by their urine, which glows bright yellow in UV light.

Killdeer
Charadrius vociferus

YEAR-ROUND
SUMMER

Size: 11" (28 cm)

Male: Upland shorebird with 2 black bands around the neck, like a necklace. Brown back and white belly. Bright reddish-orange rump, visible in flight.

Female: same as male

Juvenile: similar to adults, with a single neck band

Nest: ground; male scrapes; 2 broods per year

Eggs: 3–5; tan with brown markings

Incubation: 24–28 days; male and female incubate

Fledging: 25 days; male and female lead their young to food

Migration: non-migrator to complete, to southern states, Mexico and Central America

Food: insects, worms, snails

Compare: The Spotted Sandpiper (p. 141) is found around water but lacks the 2 neck bands of the Killdeer.

Stan's Notes: Technically classified as a shorebird but lives in dry habitats instead of the shore. Often found in vacant fields, gravel pits, driveways, wetland edges or along railroad tracks. The only shorebird that has two black neck bands. Known to fake a broken wing to draw intruders away from the nest; once the nest is safe, the parent will take flight. Nests are just a slight depression in a dry area and are often hard to see. Hatchlings look like miniature adults walking on stilts. Soon after hatching, the young follow their parents around and peck for insects. Gives a loud and distinctive "kill-deer" call. Migrates in small flocks.

male

red-shafted female

yellow-shafted male

yellow-shafted female

Northern Flicker
Colaptes auratus

YEAR-ROUND

Size: 12" (30 cm)

Male: Brown and black with a red mustache and black necklace. Speckled chest. Gray head with a brown cap. Large white rump patch, seen only when flying.

Female: same as male but without a red mustache

Juvenile: same as adult of the same sex

Nest: cavity; female and male excavate; 1 brood per year

Eggs: 5–8; white without markings

Incubation: 11–14 days; female and male incubate

Fledging: 25–28 days; female and male feed the young

Migration: non-migrator in Washington

Food: insects (especially ants and beetles); comes to suet feeders

Compare: Female Williamson's Sapsucker (p. 53) has a finely barred back with a yellow belly and lacks Flicker's black spots on chest and belly.

Stan's Notes: This is the only woodpecker to regularly feed on the ground. Prefers ants and beetles and produces an antacid saliva that neutralizes the acidic defense of ants. Can be attracted to your yard with a nest box stuffed with sawdust. Northern Flickers in western states flash reddish orange under the wings and tails when flying, while those in eastern states have golden yellow wing linings and tails. Male yellow-shafteds have black mustaches; male red-shafteds have red mustaches. Hybrids between varieties occur in the Great Plains, where ranges overlap. Often reuses an old nest. Undulates deeply during flight, flashing yellow under its wings and tail and calling "wacka-wacka" loudly.

Mourning Dove

Zenaida macroura

YEAR-ROUND
SUMMER

Size: 12" (30 cm)

Male: Smooth and fawn-colored. Gray patch on the head. Iridescent pink and greenish blue on the neck. Black spot behind and below the eyes. Black spots on the wings and tail. Pointed, wedged tail; white edges seen in flight.

Female: similar to male, but lacks the pink-and-green iridescent neck feathers

Juvenile: spotted and streaked plumage

Nest: platform; female and male build; 2 broods per year

Eggs: 2; white without markings

Incubation: 13–14 days; male incubates during the day, female incubates at night

Fledging: 12–14 days; female and male feed the young

Migration: non-migrator to partial, to southern states; will move around to find food

Food: seeds; will visit seed and ground feeders

Compare: Rock Pigeon (p. 255) is larger and has a wide range of color combinations. Band-tailed Pigeon (p. 257) is larger and has a white collar.

Stan's Notes: Name comes from its mournful cooing. A ground feeder, bobbing its head as it walks. One of the few birds to drink without lifting its head, like the Rock Pigeon (p. 255). The parents feed the young (squab) a regurgitated liquid called crop-milk for their first few days of life. Platform nest is flimsy and often falls apart in storms. During takeoff and in flight, wind rushes through the bird's wing feathers, creating a characteristic whistling sound.

winter

breeding

Pied-billed Grebe

Podilymbus podiceps

YEAR-ROUND
SUMMER

Size:	12–14" (30–36 cm)
Male:	Small and brown with a black chin and fluffy white patch beneath the tail. Black ring around a thick, chicken-like, ivory bill. Winter bill is brown and unmarked.
Female:	same as male
Juvenile:	paler than adults, with white spots and a gray chest, belly and bill
Nest:	floating platform; female and male build; 1 brood per year
Eggs:	5–7; bluish white without markings
Incubation:	22–24 days; female and male incubate
Fledging:	45–60 days; female and male feed the young
Migration:	non-migrator to partial, to southwestern states, Mexico and Central America
Food:	crayfish, aquatic insects, fish
Compare:	Look for a puffy white patch under the tail and thick, chicken-like bill to help identify.

Stan's Notes: A common resident water bird, often seen diving for food. When disturbed, it slowly sinks like a submarine, quickly compressing its feathers, forcing the air out. Was called Hell-diver due to the length of time it can stay submerged. Able to surface far from where it went under. Well suited to life on water, with short wings, lobed toes, and legs set close to the rear of its body. Swims easily but moves awkwardly on land. Very sensitive to pollution. Builds nest on a floating mat in water. "Grebe" may originate from the Breton word *krib*, meaning "crest," referring to the crested head plumes of many grebes, especially during breeding season.

male
p. 57

female

Bufflehead
Bucephala albeola

YEAR-ROUND
SUMMER
MIGRATION
WINTER

Size: 13–15" (33–38 cm)

Female: Brownish-gray duck with a dark brown head. White patch on cheek, just behind the eyes.

Male: striking black-and-white duck with a large bonnet-like white patch on the back of head; head shines greenish-purple in sunlight

Juvenile: similar to female

Nest: cavity; female lines an old woodpecker cavity; 1 brood per year

Eggs: 8–10; ivory-to-olive without markings

Incubation: 29–31 days; female incubates

Fledging: 50–55 days; female leads the young to food

Migration: complete, to southern states, Mexico and Central America; non-migrator in parts of Washington

Food: aquatic insects, crustaceans, mollusks

Compare: The female Lesser Scaup (p. 171) is slightly larger and has a white patch at the base of the bill. Look for the white cheek patch to help identify the female Bufflehead.

Stan's Notes: Common diving duck that travels with other ducks. Usually seen during migrations and winter, arriving late in August and remaining in Washington the entire winter. Most commonly found in sheltered bays and coastal harbors, it is also found inland on rivers and lakes. Nests in vacant woodpecker holes. When cavities in trees are scarce, known to use a burrow in an earthen bank or will use a nest box. Lines the cavity with fluffy down feathers. Unlike other ducks, the young stay in the nest for up to two days before they venture out with their mothers.

male

female

Green-winged Teal

Anas crecca

YEAR-ROUND

Size: 14–15" (36–38 cm)

Male: Chestnut head with a dark-green patch outlined with white from the eyes to the nape of neck. Gray body and butter-yellow tail. Green patch on the wings (speculum), seen in flight.

Female: light-brown duck with black spots and a green speculum, small bill

Juvenile: same as female

Nest: ground; female builds; 1 brood per year

Eggs: 8–10; cream-white without markings

Incubation: 21–23 days; female incubates

Fledging: 32–34 days; female teaches the young to feed

Migration: non-migrator; moves around to find food

Food: aquatic plants and insects

Compare: Male Wood Duck (p. 281) is more colorful than male Green-winged. Female Cinnamon Teal (p. 169) is similar to female Green-winged, but it has a dark line through the eyes and a larger bill. Female Blue-winged Teal (p. 167) is similar in size, but it is slightly white at the base of its bill.

Stan's Notes: One of the smallest dabbling ducks. Tips forward in water to feed off the bottom of shallow ponds. This behavior makes it vulnerable to ingesting spent lead shot, which can cause death. It walks well on land and will also feed in flooded fields and woodlands. Common year-round resident in Washington, breeding in eastern part of the state and spending the winter on the coast. The green wing patches are most obvious during flight.

male

female

Blue-winged Teal
Spatula discors

SUMMER MIGRATION

Size: 15–16" (38–41 cm)

Male: Small, plain-looking brown duck with black speckles and a large, crescent-shaped white mark at the base of the bill. Gray head. Black tail with a small white patch. Blue wing patch (speculum), best seen in flight.

Female: duller than male, with only slight white at the base of the bill; lacks a crescent mark on the face and a white patch on the tail

Juvenile: same as female

Nest: ground; female builds; 1 brood per year

Eggs: 8–11; creamy white

Incubation: 23–27 days; female incubates

Fledging: 35–44 days; female feeds the young

Migration: complete, to southwestern states, Mexico and Central America

Food: aquatic plants, seeds, aquatic insects

Compare: The female Mallard (p. 183) has an orange-and-black bill. The female Wood Duck (p. 177) has a crest. Female Green-winged Teal (p. 165) is similar in size but lacks white at base of bill. Look for the white facial mark to identify the male Blue-winged.

Stan's Notes: A common duck found mostly in eastern parts of the state. Known to hybridize with Cinnamon Teals. Constructs nest some distance from water. Female performs a distraction display to protect nest and young. Male leaves female near the end of incubation. Planting crops and cultivating to pond edges have caused a decline in population.

male

female

Cinnamon Teal
Anas cyanoptera

SUMMER
MIGRATION

Size: 15–17" (40 cm)

Male: Deep-cinnamon head, neck and belly. Light-brown back. Dark-gray bill. Deep-red eyes. Non-breeding male is overall brown with a red tinge.

Female: overall brown with a pale-brown head, long shovel-like bill, green patch on wings

Juvenile: similar to female

Nest: ground; female builds; 1 brood per year

Eggs: 7–12; pinkish white without markings

Incubation: 21–25 days; female incubates

Fledging: 40–50 days; female teaches young to feed

Migration: complete migrator, to southwestern states and Mexico

Food: aquatic plants and insects, seeds

Compare: Northern Shoveler (p. 181) also has cinnamon sides, but it is larger and has a green head and very large spoon-shaped bill. Female Green-winged Teal (p. 165) is similar to the Female Cinnamon Teal, but the Green-winged is smaller and has a dark line through its eyes.

Stan's Notes: The most common breeding teal in the state, found in low wetlands on both sides of the Cascades. The male is one of the most stunningly beautiful ducks. When threatened, the female feigns a wing injury to lure the predator away from her young. Prefers to nest along alkaline marshes and shallow lakes, within 75 yards (68 m) of the water. Mallards and other ducks often lay eggs in teal nests, resulting in many nests with over 15 eggs.

male p. 59

female

Lesser Scaup
Aythya affinis

YEAR-ROUND
SUMMER
WINTER

Size: 16–17" (40–43 cm)

Female: Overall brown duck with a dull-white patch at the base of a light-gray bill. Yellow eyes.

Male: white and gray; the chest and head appear nearly black but the head looks purple with green highlights in direct sun; yellow eyes

Juvenile: same as female

Nest: ground; female builds; 1 brood per year

Eggs: 8–14; olive-buff without markings

Incubation: 22–28 days; female incubates

Fledging: 45–50 days; female teaches young to feed

Migration: complete, to western coastal U.S., southern states, Mexico, Central America and northern South America

Food: aquatic plants and insects

Compare: Male Blue-winged Teal (p. 167) is slightly smaller and has a crescent-shaped white mark at the base of bill. Female Wood Duck (p. 177) is larger with white around eyes.

Stan's Notes: A common diving duck. Often seen in large flocks on lakes, ponds and sewage lagoons. Submerges itself completely to feed on the bottom of lakes (unlike dabbling ducks, which only tip forward to reach the bottom). Note the bold white stripe under the wings when in flight. The male leaves the female when she starts incubating eggs. The quantity of eggs (clutch size) increases with the female's age. This species has an interesting babysitting arrangement in which groups of young (crèches) are tended by one to three adult females. A rare breeder in Washington, breeding north of the state through Alaska.

female

male
p. 61

Hooded Merganser
Lophodytes cucullatus

YEAR-ROUND
SUMMER
MIGRATION
WINTER

Size:	16–19" (41–48 cm)
Female:	Sleek brown-and-rust bird with a red head. Ragged "hair" on the back of the head. Long, thin, brown bill.
Male:	black back, rust-brown sides, long black bill; raises crest "hood" to display a white patch
Juvenile:	similar to female
Nest:	cavity; female lines an old woodpecker cavity or a nest box near water; 1 brood per year
Eggs:	10–12; white without markings
Incubation:	32–33 days; female incubates
Fledging:	71 days; female feeds the young
Migration:	complete, to western coastal U.S. and Mexico; non-migrator in parts of Washington
Food:	small fish, aquatic insects, crustaceans (especially crayfish)
Compare:	Female Common Merganser (p. 287) is larger and has a white chin and a large orange bill. Female Lesser Scaup (p. 171) is smaller and has a dull-white patch at the base of its bill. Look for the ragged "hair" on the back of the head of the female Hoodie.

Stan's Notes: A small diving duck, found in shallow ponds, sloughs, lakes and rivers. Usually in small groups. Quick, low flight across the water, with fast wingbeats. Male has a deep, rolling call. Female gives a hoarse quack. Nests in wooded areas. Female will lay some eggs in the nests of other mergansers, goldeneyes or Wood Ducks (egg dumping), resulting in 20–25 eggs in some nests. Rarely, she shares a nest, sitting with a Wood Duck.

drumming

YEAR-ROUND

Ruffed Grouse
Bonasa umbellus

Size: 16–19" (41–48 cm); up to 2-ft. wingspan

Male: Brown chicken-like bird with a long, squared tail. Wide black band near tip of tail. Tuft of feathers on head (crest) appears like a crown when raised. Black ruffs on the sides of neck.

Female: same as male, but has less obvious neck ruffs

Juvenile: same as female

Nest: ground; female builds; 1 brood per year

Eggs: 9–12; tan with light brown markings

Incubation: 23–24 days; female incubates

Fledging: 10–12 days; female leads the young to food

Migration: non-migrator, moves around to find food

Food: seeds, insects, fruit, leaf buds

Compare: Female Ring-necked Pheasant (p. 203) is larger with a longer, pointed tail. Look for the feather tuft on the head and black neck ruffs to help identify the Ruffed Grouse.

Stan's Notes: A common bird of deep woods. Often seen in aspen or other trees, feeding on leaf buds. In the colder northern climates, scaly bristles grow on its feet during winter and serve as snowshoes. When there is enough snow, it dives into a snowbank to roost at night. In spring, the male attracts females by raising its feather tuft, fanning its tail like a turkey and standing on a log, drumming with its wings. The drumming sound is not made by its wings pounding against its chest or hitting the log, but by the air being moved by its cupped wings. Female performs a distraction display to protect her young. Two color morphs, red and gray, most apparent in the tail. Named for the black ruffs on its neck.

male
p. 281

female

Wood Duck

Aix sponsa

**YEAR-ROUND
SUMMER**

Size: 17–20" (43–51 cm)

Female: Small brown dabbling duck. Bright-white eye-ring and a not-so-obvious crest. Blue patch on wings (speculum), often hidden.

Male: highly ornamented, with a mostly green head and crest patterned with black and white; rusty chest, white belly and red eyes

Juvenile: similar to female

Nest: cavity; female lines an old woodpecker cavity or a nest box in a tree; 1 brood per year

Eggs: 10–15; creamy white without markings

Incubation: 28–36 days; female incubates

Fledging: 56–68 days; female teaches the young to feed

Migration: complete, to southwestern states; partial to non-migrator in parts of Washington

Food: aquatic insects, plants, seeds

Compare: The female Mallard (p. 183) and female Blue-winged Teal (p. 167) lack the eye-ring and crest. The female Northern Shoveler (p. 181) is larger and has a large spoon-shaped bill.

Stan's Notes: A common duck of quiet, shallow backwater ponds. Nearly went extinct around 1900 due to overhunting, but it's doing well now. Nests in a tree cavity or a nest box in a tree. Seen flying in forests or perching on high branches. Female takes off with a loud, squealing call and enters the nest cavity from full flight. Lays some eggs in a neighboring nest (egg dumping), resulting in more than 20 eggs in some clutches. Hatchlings stay in the nest for 24 hours, then jump from as high as 60 feet (18 m) to the ground or water to follow their mother. They never return to the nest.

male

female

American Wigeon
Anas americana

YEAR-ROUND
SUMMER

Size: 18–20" (48 cm)

Male: Brown duck with a rounded head and obvious white cap. Deep-green patch starting behind the eyes and streaking down the neck. Long pointed tail. Short, black-tipped grayish bill. White belly and wing linings, seen in flight. Non-breeding lacks white cap and green patch.

Female: light brown with a pale-gray head, a short, black-tipped grayish bill, green wing patch (speculum) and dark eye spot; white belly and wing linings, seen in flight

Juvenile: similar to female

Nest: ground; female builds; 1 brood per year

Eggs: 7–12; white without markings

Incubation: 23–25 days; female incubates

Fledging: 37–48 days; female teaches the young to feed

Migration: partial migrator to non-migrator

Food: aquatic plants, seeds

Compare: Male American Wigeon is easily identified by the white cap and black-tipped grayish bill. Female Wigeon is similar to the female Cinnamon Teal (p. 169), but Wigeon has a short black-tipped bill and is less common.

Stan's Notes: Often in small flocks or with other ducks. Prefers shallow lakes. Male stays with the female only during the first week of incubation. Female raises the young. If threatened, female feigns injury while the young run and hide. Conceals upland nest in tall vegetation within 50–250 yards (46–229 m) of water. Winters on the West Coast.

male p. 285

female

Northern Shoveler
Anas clypeata

YEAR-ROUND
SUMMER

Size: 19–21" (48–53 cm)

Female: A medium-sized brown duck speckled with black. Green patch on the wings (speculum). An extraordinarily large, spoon-shaped bill.

Male: iridescent green head, rusty sides, white chest and a large spoon-shaped bill

Juvenile: same as female

Nest: ground; female builds; 1 brood per year

Eggs: 9–12; olive without markings

Incubation: 22–25 days; female incubates

Fledging: 30–60 days; female leads the young to food

Migration: non-migrator to partial migrator, to south-western states, Mexico and Central America

Food: aquatic insects, plants

Compare: Female Mallard (p. 183) is similar but lacks the Shoveler's large bill. Female Wood Duck (p. 177) is smaller and has a white eye-ring. Look for Shoveler's large spoon-shaped bill to help identify.

Stan's Notes: One of several species of shovelers. Called "Shoveler" due to the peculiar, shovel-like shape of its bill. Given the common name "Northern" because it is the only species of these ducks in North America. Seen in shallow wetlands, ponds and small lakes in flocks of 5–10 birds. Flocks fly in tight formation. Swims low in water, pointing its large bill toward the water as if it's too heavy to lift. Usually swims in tight circles while feeding. Feeds mainly by filtering tiny aquatic insects and plants from the surface of the water with its bill.

181

male
p. 283

female

Mallard
Anas platyrhynchos

YEAR-ROUND

Size: 19–21" (48–53 cm)

Female: Brown duck with a blue-and-white wing mark (speculum). Orange-and-black bill.

Male: large green head, white necklace, rust-brown or chestnut chest, combination of gray-and-white sides, yellow bill, orange legs and feet

Juvenile: same as female but with a yellow bill

Nest: ground; female builds; 1 brood per year

Eggs: 7–10; greenish to whitish, unmarked

Incubation: 26–30 days; female incubates

Fledging: 42–52 days; female leads the young to food

Migration: partial to non-migrator in Washington

Food: seeds, plants, aquatic insects; will come to ground feeders offering corn

Compare: Female Gadwall (p. 185) has a gray bill with orange sides, unlike female Mallard's orange and black bill. Female Northern Shoveler (p. 181) has a spoon-shaped bill. Female Wood Duck (p. 177) has a white eye-ring.

Stan's Notes: A familiar dabbling duck of lakes and ponds. Also found in rivers, streams and some backyards. Tips forward to feed on vegetation on the bottom of shallow water. The name "Mallard" comes from the Latin word *masculus,* meaning "male," referring to the male's habit of taking no part in raising the young. Female and male have white underwings and white tails, but only the male has black central tail feathers that curl upward. The female gives a classic quack. Returns to its birthplace each year.

male
p. 265

female

Gadwall
Mareca strepera

YEAR-ROUND

Size: 19" (48 cm)

Female: Mottled brown with a pronounced color change from dark-brown body to light-brown neck and head. Bright-white wing linings, seen in flight. Small white wing patch, seen when swimming. Gray bill with orange sides.

Male: plump gray duck with a brown head and distinctive black rump, white belly, bright-white wing linings, small white wing patch, chestnut-tinged wings, gray bill

Juvenile: similar to female

Nest: ground; female lines the nest with fine grass and down feathers plucked from her chest; 1 brood per year

Eggs: 8–11; white without markings

Incubation: 24–27 days; female incubates

Fledging: 48–56 days; young feed themselves

Migration: non-migrator; moves around to find food

Food: aquatic insects

Compare: Female Mallard (p. 183) is similar but has a blue-and-white wing mark. Look for Gadwall's white wing patch and gray bill with orange sides.

Stan's Notes: A duck of shallow marshes. Found in freshwater wetlands in eastern Washington but most common in the southern part of Puget Sound. Consumes mostly plant material, dunking its head in water to feed rather than tipping forward. Walks well on land; feeds in fields and woodlands. Nests within 300 feet (90 m) of water. Establishes pair bond during winter.

male

female

YEAR-ROUND
SUMMER
WINTER

Northern Pintail
Anas acuta

Size: 25" (63 cm), male
20" (52 cm), female

Male: A slender, elegant duck with a brown head, white neck and gray body. Gray bill. Extremely long and narrow black tail. Non-breeding has a pale-brown head that lacks the clear demarcation between the brown head and white neck. Lacks long tail feathers.

Female: mottled brown body with a paler head and neck, long tail, gray bill

Juvenile: similar to female

Nest: ground; female builds; 1 brood per year

Eggs: 6–9; olive-green without markings

Incubation: 22–25 days; female incubates

Fledging: 36–50 days; female teaches young to feed

Migration: non-migrator to partial migrator

Food: aquatic plants and insects, seeds

Compare: The male Northern Pintail has a distinctive brown head and white neck and unique long tail feathers. Female Mallard (p. 183) is similar to female Pintail, but Mallard has an orange bill with black spots.

Stan's Notes: A common dabbling duck of marshes. About 90 percent of its diet is aquatic plants, except when females feed heavily on aquatic insects prior to nesting, presumably to gain extra nutrients for egg production. Male holds tail upright from the water's surface. No other North American duck has such a long tail.

male
p. 263

female

soaring

YEAR-ROUND SUMMER

Northern Harrier
Circus hudsonius

Size: 18–22" (45–56 cm); up to 4' wingspan

Female: Slender, low-flying hawk with a dark-brown back and brown streaking on the chest and belly. Large white rump patch. Thin black tail bands and black wing tips. Yellow eyes.

Male: silver-gray with a large white rump patch and white belly, black wing tips, yellow eyes, faint, thin bands across the tail

Juvenile: similar to female, with an orange breast

Nest: ground; female and male construct; 1 brood per year

Eggs: 4–8; bluish white without markings

Incubation: 31–32 days; female incubates

Fledging: 30–35 days; male and female feed the young

Migration: non-migrator to partial migrator

Food: mice, snakes, insects, small birds

Compare: Slimmer than the Red-tailed Hawk (p. 195). Look for the characteristic low gliding and the black tail bands to identify the female Harrier.

Stan's Notes: One of the easiest of hawks to identify. Glides just above the ground, following the contours of the land while searching for prey. Holds its wings just above horizontal, tilting back and forth in the wind, similar to the Turkey Vulture. Formerly called Marsh Hawk due to its habit of hunting over marshes. Feeds and nests on the ground. Will also preen and rest on the ground. Unlike other hawks, mainly uses its hearing to find prey, followed by its sight. At any age, it has a distinctive owl-like face disk.

dark
morph

soaring dark
morph

light morph

soaring light
morph

Rough-legged Hawk

Buteo lagopus

WINTER

Size: 18–23" (56 cm); up to 4½' wingspan

Male: A hawk of several plumages. All plumages have a long tail with a dark band or bands. Distinctive dark wrists and belly. Relatively long wings, small bill and feet. Light morph has nearly pure white undersides of wings and base of tail. Dark morph is nearly all brown with light-gray trailing edge of wings.

Female: same as male, only larger

Juvenile: same as adults

Nest: platform, on edge of cliff; female and male build; 1 brood per year

Eggs: 2–6; white without markings

Incubation: 28–31 days; female and male incubate

Fledging: 39–43 days; female and male feed young

Migration: complete, to the northern half of the U.S.

Food: small animals, snakes, large insects

Compare: Similar size as Swainson's Hawk (p. 193), which has narrow pointed wings, as seen in flight, and a lighter leading edge of wings unlike Rough-legged's lighter trailing edge of wings.

Stan's Notes: Two color morphs, light and dark, light being more common. Common winter resident, nesting in Canada's Northwest Territories and Alaska. More numerous in some years than others. It has much smaller and weaker feet than the other birds of prey, which means it must hunt smaller prey. Hunts from the air, usually hovering before diving for small rodents such as mice and voles.

soaring light morph

intermediate morph

light morph

dark morph

soaring dark morph

Swainson's Hawk
Buteo swainsoni

SUMMER

Size: 19–22" (48–56 cm); up to 4¾' wingspan

Male: Highly variable plumage with three easily distinguishable color morphs. Light morph is brown and has a white belly, warm rusty chest and white face. Intermediate has a dark chest, rusty belly and white at the base of bill. Dark morph is nearly all dark brown with a rusty color low on the belly.

Female: same as male

Juvenile: similar to adult

Nest: platform; female and male construct; 1 brood per year

Eggs: 2–4; bluish or white with some brown marks

Incubation: 28–35 days; female and male incubate

Fledging: 28–30 days; female and male feed young

Migration: complete, to Central and South America

Food: small mammals, insects, snakes, birds

Compare: Slimmer than Red-tailed Hawk (p. 195) which has a white chest and brown belly band. Swainson's Hawk has longer, more pointed wings and a longer tail. Rough-legged Hawk (p. 191) has a lighter trailing edge of wings.

Stan's Notes: A slender open country hawk that hunts mammals, insects, snakes and birds when soaring (kiting) or perching. Often flies with slightly upturned wings in a teetering, vulture-like flight. The light morph is the most common, but the intermediate and dark are also common. Even minor nest disturbance can cause nest failure. Often gathers in large flocks to migrate.

Western

soaring

Eastern

soaring

juvenile
soaring

juvenile

Red-tailed Hawk

Buteo jamaicensis

YEAR-ROUND

Size: 19–23" (48–63 cm); up to 4½' wingspan

Male: Variety of colorations, from chocolate brown to nearly all white. Often brown with a white breast and brown belly band. Rust-red tail. Underside of wing is white with a small dark patch on the leading edge near the shoulder.

Female: same as male but slightly larger

Juvenile: similar to adults, with a speckled breast and light eyes; lacks a red tail

Nest: platform; male and female build; 1 brood per year

Eggs: 2–3; white without markings or sometimes marked with brown

Incubation: 30–35 days; female and male incubate

Fledging: 45–46 days; male and female feed the young

Migration: non-migrator to partial migrator

Food: small and medium-sized animals, large birds, snakes, fish, insects, bats, carrion

Compare: Swainson's Hawk (p. 193) is slimmer with longer, more pointed wings and longer tail.

Stan's Notes: Common in open country and cities. Seen perching on fences, freeway lampposts and trees. Look for it circling above open fields and roadsides, searching for prey. Gives a high-pitched scream that trails off. Often builds a large stick nest in large trees along roads. Lines nest with finer material, like evergreen needles. Returns to the same nest site each year. The red tail develops in the second year and is best seen from above. Western variety has a brown chin, while Eastern has a white chin. Map reflects the combined range.

Barred Owl
Strix varia

YEAR-ROUND

Size: 20–24" (51–61 cm); up to 3½' wingspan

Male: Chunky brown-and-gray owl. Dark horizontal barring on upper chest. Vertical streaks on lower chest and belly. A large head and dark-brown eyes. Yellow bill and feet.

Female: same as male but slightly larger

Juvenile: light gray with a black face

Nest: cavity; does not add any nesting material; 1 brood per year

Eggs: 2–3; white without markings

Incubation: 28–33 days; female incubates

Fledging: 42–44 days; female and male feed the young

Migration: non-migrator

Food: mice, rabbits and other animals; small birds; fish; reptiles; amphibians

Compare: Great Horned Owl (p. 199) has horns, and the much smaller Western Screech-Owl (p. 237) has ears, both of which Barred Owl lacks. Look for a stocky owl with a large head and dark-brown eyes to identify the Barred Owl.

Stan's Notes: Prefers deciduous woodlands but can be attracted to your yard with a simple nest box that has a large entrance hole. Often seen hunting during the day. Perches and watches for mice, birds and other prey. Hovers over water and reaches down to grab fish. After fledging, the young stay with the parents for up to four months. Often sounds like a dog barking before calling six to eight hoots, sounding like "who-who-who-cooks-for-you."

Great Horned Owl

Bubo virginianus

YEAR-ROUND

Size: 21–25" (53–64 cm); up to 4' wingspan

Male: Robust brown "horned" owl. Bright-yellow eyes and a V-shaped white throat resembling a necklace. Horizontal barring on the chest.

Female: same as male but slightly larger

Juvenile: similar to adults but lacks ear tufts

Nest: no nest; takes over the nest of a crow, hawk or Great Blue Heron or uses a partial cavity, stump or broken tree; 1 brood per year

Eggs: 2–3; white without markings

Incubation: 26–30 days; female incubates

Fledging: 30–35 days; male and female feed the young

Migration: non-migrator

Food: mammals, birds (ducks), snakes, insects

Compare: Barred Owl (p. 197) has dark eyes and no "horns." The Western Screech-Owl (p. 237) is extremely tiny. Look for bright-yellow eyes and feather "horns" on the head to help identify the Great Horned Owl.

Stan's Notes: One of the earliest nesting birds in the state, laying eggs in January and February. Able to hunt in complete darkness due to its excellent hearing. The "horns," or "ears," are tufts of feathers and have nothing to do with hearing. Cannot turn its head all the way around. Wing feathers are ragged on the ends, resulting in silent flight. Eyelids close from the top down, like humans. Fearless, it is one of the few animals that will kill skunks and porcupines. Given that, it is also called the Flying Tiger. Call sounds like "hoo-hoo-hoo-hoooo."

cinnamon
wing linings

Long-billed Curlew
Numenius americanus

SUMMER
MIGRATION
WINTER

Size: 23" (58 cm), including bill

Male: Cinnamon brown with an extremely long, down-curved bill. Long bluish legs. Darker cinnamon wing linings.

Female: same as male, but with a longer bill

Juvenile: same as adults, but with a shorter bill

Nest: ground; female builds; 1 brood per year

Eggs: 5–7; olive-green with brown markings

Incubation: 27–30 days; female and male incubate, the female during day, male at night

Fledging: 32–45 days; female and male feed young

Migration: complete, to West Coast states, Central and South American coasts

Food: insects, worms, crabs, eggs

Compare: Spotted Sandpiper (p. 141) is smaller, less than half the size of Long-billed Curlew. Hard to mistake the exceptionally long bill.

Stan's Notes: The largest of shorebirds, with an appropriate name. The extremely long bill is greater than half the length of its body. Female has a longer bill than male. Juvenile has a short bill, which grows into a long bill during the first six months. Uses bill to probe deep into mud for insects and worms. Female incubates during the day, male during the night. Although a shorebird, it is often in grass fields away from the shore. Breeds in open valleys and flatlands. Will fly up to 6 miles (10 km) from nest site to find food. Arrives in Washington in April to begin nesting. Decreasing in Washington due to human activities, which destroy its nesting habitat.

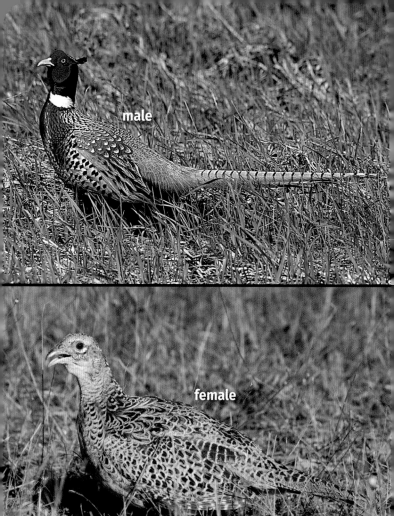

Ring-necked Pheasant
Phasianus colchicus

YEAR-ROUND

Size:	30–36" (76–91 cm), male, including tail 21–25" (53–64 cm), female, including tail
Male:	Golden-brown body with a long tail. White ring around the neck. Head is purple, green, blue and red.
Female:	smaller and less flamboyant than the male, with brown plumage and a long tail
Juvenile:	similar to female, with a shorter tail
Nest:	ground; female builds; 1 brood per year
Eggs:	8–10; olive brown without markings
Incubation:	23–25 days; female incubates
Fledging:	11–12 days; female leads the young to food
Migration:	non-migrator
Food:	insects, seeds, fruit; visits ground feeders
Compare:	California Quail (p. 247) is much smaller and has a teardrop plume on the forehead. Male Ring-necked is brightly colored.

Stan's Notes: Originally introduced to North America from China in the late 1800s. Common now throughout the U.S. Like many other game birds, its numbers vary greatly, making it common in some years, scarce in others. Seeks shelter during harsh winter weather. To attract females, the male gives a cackling call and then rapidly flutters his wings. Takes off in an explosive flight with fast wingbeats followed by gliding low to the ground. The name "Ring-necked" refers to the white ring around the male's neck. "Pheasant" comes from the Greek word *phaisianos*, which means "bird of the River Phasis" (known today as the Rioni River).

soaring

juvenile

juvenile

Golden Eagle
Aquila chrysaetos

Size: 30–40" (76–102 cm); up to 7¼' wingspan

Male: Uniform dark brown with a golden-yellow head and nape of neck. Yellow around base of bill. Yellow feet.

Female: same as male

Juvenile: similar to adult, with white "wrist" patches and a white base of tail

Nest: platform, on a cliff; female and male build; 1 brood per year

Eggs: 1–2; white with brown markings

Incubation: 43–45 days; female and male incubate

Fledging: 63–75 days; female and male feed young

Migration: non-migrator to partial migrator; moves around to find food

Food: mammals, birds, reptiles, insects

Compare: The Bald Eagle (p. 75) adult is similar, but it has a white head and white tail. Bald Eagle juvenile is often confused with the Golden Eagle juvenile; both are large dark birds with white markings.

Stan's Notes: A large, powerful raptor that has no trouble taking larger prey such as jackrabbits. Hunts by perching or soaring and watching for movement. Inhabits mountainous terrain, requiring large territories to provide a large supply of food. Long-term pair bond, renewing its bond late in winter with spectacular high-flying courtship displays. Usually nests on cliff faces; rarely nests in trees. Uses a well-established nest that's been used for generations. Will add items to the nest such as antlers, bones and barbed wire.

displaying male

non-displaying

female

Wild Turkey
Meleagris gallopavo

YEAR-ROUND

Size: 36–48" (91–122 cm)

Male: Large brown-and-bronze bird with a naked blue-and-red head. Long, straight, black beard in the center of the chest. Tail spreads open like a fan. Spurs on legs.

Female: thinner and less striking than the male; often lacks a breast beard

Juvenile: same as adult of the same sex

Nest: ground; female builds; 1 brood per year

Eggs: 10–12; buff-white with dull-brown markings

Incubation: 27–28 days; female incubates

Fledging: 6–10 days; female leads the young to food

Migration: non-migrator; moves around to find food

Food: insects, seeds, fruit

Compare: This bird is quite distinctive and unlikely to be confused with others.

Stan's Notes: The largest native game bird in the state, and the species from which the domestic turkey was bred. A strong flier that can approach 60 miles (97 km) per hour. Can fly straight up, then away. Eyesight is three times better than ours. Hearing is also excellent; can hear competing males up to a mile away. Male has a "harem" of up to 20 females. Female scrapes out a shallow depression for nesting and pads it with soft leaves. Males are known as toms, females are hens, and young are poults. Roosts in trees at night. Eliminated from many states by the turn of the 20th century due to market hunting and loss of habitat. Populations were later reintroduced and are now stable.

non-breeding

chick-feeding
adult

breeding

in flight

juvenile

Brown Pelican
Pelecanus occidentalis

MIGRATION

Size: 46–50" (117–127 cm); up to 7' wingspan

Male: Brown-gray body with a black belly and an exceptionally long bill. Breeding has a white or yellow head, dark chestnut hind neck and a bright red expandable throat pouch. Non-breeding has a white head and neck and a gray throat pouch.

Female: similar to male

Juvenile: brown with white breast and belly; does not acquire adult plumage until the third year

Nest: ground; female and male build; 1 brood per year

Eggs: 2–4; white without markings

Incubation: 28–30 days; female and male incubate

Fledging: 71–86 days; female and male feed the young

Migration: complete, to southern California, Mexico

Food: fish

Compare: Unmistakable bird in Washington.

Stan's Notes: A coastal bird of Washington and recently was an endangered species. Suffering from eggshell thinning in the 1970s due to DDT and other pesticides, it is now reestablishing along the East, Gulf and West Coasts. Captures fish by diving headfirst into the ocean, opening its large bill and "netting" fish with its gular pouch. Often seen sitting on posts around marinas. Nests in large colonies. Doesn't breed before the age of 3, when it obtains its breeding plumage. The Pacific variety (shown) has a bright-red throat pouch unlike the brown patch of the Atlantic and Gulf Coast birds.

Ruby-crowned Kinglet
Regulus calendula

YEAR-ROUND
SUMMER
WINTER

Size: 4" (10 cm)

Male: Small, teardrop-shaped green-to-gray bird. Two white wing bars and a white eye-ring. Hidden ruby crown.

Female: same as male, but lacks a ruby crown

Juvenile: same as female

Nest: pendulous; female builds; 1 brood per year

Eggs: 4–5; white with brown markings

Incubation: 11–12 days; female incubates

Fledging: 11–12 days; female and male feed the young

Migration: partial to non-migrator in Washington

Food: insects, berries

Compare: Golden-crowned Kinglet (p. 213) is similar, but its crown is yellow to orange. The female American Goldfinch (p. 325) shares the drab-olive plumage and unmarked chest, but it is larger. Look for the white eye-ring to identify the Ruby-crowned Kinglet.

Stan's Notes: One of the smaller birds in the state. Look for it flitting around thick, low shrubs. It takes a quick eye to see the ruby crown, which the male flashes when excited. The female weaves an unusually intricate nest and fastens colorful lichens and mosses to the exterior with spiderwebs. Often builds the nest high in a mature tree, hanging from a branch that has overlapping leaves. Sings a distinctive song that starts out soft and ends loud and on a higher note. "Kinglet" originates from the word king, referring to the male's red crown, and the diminutive suffix let, meaning "small."

male

female

Golden-crowned Kinglet

Regulus satrapa

YEAR-ROUND
WINTER

Size: 4" (10 cm)

Male: Tiny, plump green-to-gray bird. Distinctive yellow-and-orange patch with a black border on the crown (see inset). A white eyebrow mark. Two white wing bars.

Female: same as male, but has a yellow crown with a black border, lacks any orange (see inset)

Juvenile: same as adults, but lacks gold on the crown

Nest: pendulous; female constructs; 1–2 broods per year

Eggs: 5–9; white or creamy with brown markings

Incubation: 14–15 days; female incubates

Fledging: 14–19 days; female and male feed young

Migration: non-migrator to partial in Washington

Food: insects, fruit, tree sap

Compare: Similar to Ruby-crowned Kinglet (p. 211), but Golden-crowned has an obvious crown. Smaller than the female American Goldfinch (p. 325), which has an all-black forehead.

Stan's Notes: Common year-round resident in much of the state, but might be more frequently seen during migration when flocks from farther north move through Washington. Often seen in flocks with chickadees, nuthatches, woodpeckers, Brown Creepers and Ruby-crowned Kinglets. Flicks its wings when moving around. Constructs an unusual hanging nest, often with moss, lichens and spiderwebs, and lines it with bark and feathers. Can have so many eggs in its small nest that eggs are in two layers. Drinks tree sap and feeds by gleaning insects from trees.

Pygmy Nuthatch
Sitta pygmaea

YEAR-ROUND

Size: 4¼" (10.5 cm)

Male: Tiny gray-blue and black bird with gray-brown crown. Creamy chest with a lighter chin. A relatively short tail, large head and long bill.

Female: same as male

Juvenile: same as adult

Nest: cavity; female and male construct; 1 brood per year

Eggs: 4–8; white with brown markings

Incubation: 14–16 days; female incubates

Fledging: 20–22 days; female and male feed young

Migration: non-migrator

Food: insects, berries, seeds; will visit seed feeders

Compare: Red-breasted Nuthatch (p. 217) is larger and has a rusty-red chest. White-breasted Nuthatch (p. 227) is larger and has a distinctive black cap and a white chest.

Stan's Notes: A bird of Ponderosa Pine forest along the eastern side of the Cascades. Unlike the White-breasted Nuthatch, the Pygmy Nuthatch requires mature pines with old or decaying wood. Usually drills its own nest cavity. While it does not migrate, it forms winter flocks with chickadees and other birds and moves around to find food. Usually feeds in the crown of a tree or at the ends of twigs and branches, where it searches for insects and seeds. This is unlike White-breasted and Red-breasted Nuthatches, which usually search trunks of trees for food.

Red-breasted Nuthatch

Sitta canadensis

YEAR-ROUND WINTER

Size: 4½" (11 cm)

Male: Gray-backed bird with an obvious black eye line and black cap. Rust-red breast and belly.

Female: duller than male and has a gray cap and pale undersides

Juvenile: same as female

Nest: cavity; male and female excavate a cavity or move into a vacant hole; 1 brood per year

Eggs: 5–6; white with red-brown markings

Incubation: 11–12 days; female incubates

Fledging: 14–20 days; female and male feed the young

Migration: non-migrator to irruptive; moves around the state in search of food

Food: insects, insect eggs, seeds; comes to seed and suet feeders

Compare: Pygmy Nuthatch (p. 215) is slightly smaller with a creamy chest. The White-breasted Nuthatch (p. 227) is larger and has a white breast. Look for Red-breasted's rust-red breast and black eye line.

Stan's Notes: The nuthatch climbs down trunks of trees headfirst, searching for insects. Like a chickadee, it grabs a seed from a feeder and flies off to crack it open. Wedges the seed into a crevice and pounds it open with several sharp blows. The name "Nuthatch" comes from the Middle English moniker *nuthak*, referring to the habit of hacking seeds open. Look for it in mature conifers, where it extracts seeds from pine cones. Excavates a cavity or takes an old woodpecker hole or a natural cavity and builds a nest within. Gives a series of nasal "yank-yank-yank" calls.

Bushtit
Psaltriparus minimus

YEAR-ROUND

Size: 4½" (11 cm)

Male: Dull gray with a slightly brown cap. Relatively long tail. Black eyes and legs. Tiny black bill.

Female: same as male, but has pale-yellow eyes

Juvenile: similar to adults, with dark-brown eyes

Nest: pendulous; female and male construct; 1–2 broods per year

Eggs: 5–7; white without markings

Incubation: 10–12 days; female and male incubate

Fledging: 14–15 days; female and male feed the young

Migration: non-migrator

Food: insects, seeds, fruit; comes to seed feeders

Compare: Black-capped (p. 221), Mountain (p, 223) and Chestnut-backed (p. 93) Chickadees are larger, have black crowns and white on their faces.

Stan's Notes: A lively bird, often seen in extended family flocks of up to 20 individuals in open woods and low woodlands. It is often seen with other bird species, such as kinglets, wrens and chickadees. Easily picked out by its small size, long tail and the extremely short bill. Groups will roost together, huddling tightly to keep warm and save energy. Eyes are pale yellow in adult females, dark brown in juveniles and black in adult males. Away from the coast, adults lack the brown cap, appearing all dull gray.

Black-capped Chickadee
Poecile atricapillus

YEAR-ROUND

Size: 5" (13 cm)

Male: Familiar gray bird with a black cap and throat patch. Tan sides and belly. White chest. Small white wing marks.

Female: same as male

Juvenile: same as adult

Nest: cavity; female and male excavate or use a nest box; 1 brood per year

Eggs: 5–7; white with fine brown markings

Incubation: 11–13 days; female and male incubate

Fledging: 14–18 days; female and male feed the young

Migration: non-migrator

Food: insects, seeds, fruit; comes to seed and suet feeders

Compare: Mountain Chickadee (p. 223) has white eyebrows. Chestnut-backed Chickadee (p. 93) has a distinctive chestnut color.

Stan's Notes: A perky backyard bird that can be attracted with a nest box or bird feeder. Usually the first to find a new seed or suet feeder. Can be easily tamed and hand fed. Much of the diet comes from bird feeders, so it can be a common urban bird. Needs to feed every day in winter and forages to find food even during the worst winter storms. Typically seen with nuthatches, woodpeckers and other birds. Builds nest mostly with green moss and lines it with fur. Named "Chickadee" for its familiar "chika-dee-dee-dee-dee" call. Also gives a high-pitched, two-toned "fee-bee" call. Can have different calls in different regions.

YEAR-ROUND

Mountain Chickadee
Poecile gambeli

Size: 5½" (14 cm)

Male: Gray overall with a black cap, chin and line through the eyes. White eyebrows.

Female: same as male

Juvenile: similar to adult

Nest: cavity, old woodpecker hole or excavates its own; female and male build; 1–2 broods per year

Eggs: 5–8; white without markings

Incubation: 11–14 days; female and male incubate

Fledging: 18–21 days; female and male feed the young

Migration: non-migrator; moves around to find food

Food: seeds, insects; visits seed and suet feeders

Compare: The Black-capped Chickadee (p. 221) is similar, but it lacks the white eyebrows of the Mountain Chickadee. Bushtit (p. 219) is smaller and lacks the black cap and white on face.

Stan's Notes: An abundant bird in the state, but more common in coniferous forests in northeastern Washington. Prefers old-growth spruce, fir and Lodgepole Pine forests. Feeds heavily on coniferous seeds and insects. Usually will not mingle with Black-capped Chickadees, but does flock with other birds during winter. Moves to lower elevations in winter, returning to high elevations for nesting. Excavates a nest cavity or uses an old woodpecker hole. Will use a nest box. Occasionally uses the same nest site year after year. Lines its nest with moss, hair and feathers. Female will not leave her nest if disturbed, but will hiss and flutter wings.

female
p. 109

male

Oregon
male

Dark-eyed Junco

Junco hyemalis

YEAR-ROUND
WINTER

Size: 5½" (14 cm)

Male: Plump, dark-eyed bird with a slate-gray-to-charcoal chest, head and back. White belly. Pink bill. White outer tail feathers appear like a white V in flight.

Female: round with brown plumage

Juvenile: similar to female, with streaking on the breast and head

Nest: cup; female and male build; 2 broods per year

Eggs: 3–5; white with reddish brown markings

Incubation: 12–13 days; female incubates

Fledging: 10–13 days; male and female feed the young

Migration: non-migrator to partial migrator

Food: seeds, insects; visits ground and seed feeders

Compare: Rarely confused with any other bird. Look for the pink bill and small flocks feeding under feeders to identify the male Dark-eyed Junco.

Stan's Notes: A common year-round resident. A common and widespread nester in forested areas of the state. Very common in most cities during winter, rare during nesting season. Nests in a wide variety of wooded habitats in April and May. Adheres to a rigid social hierarchy, with dominant birds chasing the less dominant birds. Look for the white outer tail feathers flashing in flight. Often seen in small flocks on the ground, where it uses its feet to simultaneously "double-scratch" to expose seeds and insects. Eats many weed seeds. Several subspecies of Dark-eyed Junco were previously considered to be separate species (see lower inset).

White-breasted Nuthatch
Sitta carolinensis

YEAR-ROUND

Size: 5–6" (13–15 cm)

Male: Slate gray with a white face, breast and belly. Large white patch on the rump. Black cap and nape. Bill is long and thin, slightly upturned. Chestnut undertail.

Female: similar to male, but has a gray cap and nape

Juvenile: similar to female

Nest: cavity; female and male build a nest within; 1 brood per year

Eggs: 5–7; white with brown markings

Incubation: 11–12 days; female incubates

Fledging: 13–14 days; female and male feed the young

Migration: non-migrator

Food: insects, insect eggs, seeds; comes to seed and suet feeders

Compare: Red-breasted Nuthatch (p. 217) is smaller and has a rust-red belly and distinctive black eye line. Pygmy Nuthatch (p. 215) is smaller and lacks the White-breasted's black cap.

Stan's Notes: The nuthatch hops headfirst down trees, looking for insects missed by birds climbing up. Its climbing agility is due to an extra-long hind toe claw, or nail, that is nearly twice the size of its front claws. "Nuthatch," from the Middle English *nuthak*, refers to the bird's habit of wedging a seed in a crevice and hacking it open. Often seen in flocks with Brown Creepers, chickadees and Downy Woodpeckers. Mates stay together year-round, defending a small territory. Gives a characteristic "whi-whi-whi-whi" spring call during February and March. One of nearly 30 worldwide nuthatch species.

male

female

Yellow-rumped Warbler
Setophaga coronata

Size: 5–6" (13–15 cm)

Male: Slate gray with black streaking on the chest. Yellow patches on the head, flanks and rump. White chin and belly. Two white wing bars.

Female: duller gray than the male, mixed with brown

Juvenile: first winter is similar to the adult female

Nest: cup; female builds; 2 broods per year

Eggs: 4–5; white with brown markings

Incubation: 12–13 days; female incubates

Fledging: 10–12 days; female and male feed young

Migration: complete, to southern states, Mexico and Central America; non-migrator in western Washington

Food: insects, berries; visits suet feeders in spring

Compare: The male Wilson's Warbler (p. 323) has a black cap. The male Yellow Warbler (p. 331) is yellow with orange streaks on breast. Common Yellowthroat (p. 327) has a yellow chest and black mask. Look for patches of yellow on the rump, head, flanks and chin of Yellow-rumped Warbler to help identify.

Stan's Notes: Nests in coniferous and aspen forests. Most migrate, but in some years many can be found along the coast in the winter. Familiar call is a single robust "chip," heard mostly during migration. Sings a wonderful song in spring. In the fall, the male molts to a dull color similar to the female, but he retains his yellow patches all year. Frequently called Audubon's Warbler in western states and Myrtle Warbler in eastern states. Sometimes called Butter-butt due to the yellow patch on its rump.

Western Wood-Pewee
Contopus sordidulus

SUMMER

Size: 6¼" (15.5 cm)

Male: An overall gray bird with darker wings and tail. Two narrow gray wing bars. Dull-white throat with pale-yellow or white belly. Black upper bill, dull-orange lower.

Female: same as male

Juvenile: similar to adult, lacking the two-toned bill

Nest: cup; female builds; 1 brood per year

Eggs: 2–4; pale white with brown markings

Incubation: 12–14 days; female incubates

Fledging: 14–18 days; female and male feed young

Migration: complete, to Central and South America

Food: insects

Compare: This is an unremarkable bird. Look for the Wood-Pewee's distinctive gray wing bars to help identify it.

Stan's Notes: A widespread bird in the state that is most common in aspen forests and near water. It requires trees with dead tops or branches from which to sing and hunt for flying insects, which compose nearly all of the diet. Often returns to the same perch after each foray. Nests throughout western North America from Alaska to Mexico. Populations have been decreasing over recent years. Common name comes from its nasal whistle, "pee-wee."

American Dipper

Cinclus mexicanus

YEAR-ROUND

Size: 7½" (19 cm)

Male: Dark gray to black overall. Head is slightly lighter in color. Short upturned tail. Dark eyes and bill.

Female: same as male

Juvenile: similar to adult, only paler with white eyelids that are most noticeable when blinking

Nest: pendulous, covered nest with the entrance near the bottom, on cliff, behind waterfall; female builds; 1–2 broods per year

Eggs: 3–5; white without markings

Incubation: 13–17 days; female incubates

Fledging: 18–25 days; female and male feed young

Migration: non-migrator; seeks moving open water

Food: aquatic insects, small fish, crustaceans

Compare: American Robin (p. 245) is a similar shape, but it has a red breast. American Dipper is the only songbird in the state that dives into fast-moving water.

Stan's Notes: A common bird of fast, usually noisy streams that provide some kind of protected shelf on which to construct a nest. Some have had success attracting with man-made ledges. Plunges headfirst into fast-moving water, looking for just about any aquatic insect, propelling itself underwater with its wings. Frequently seen emerging with a large insect, which it smashes against rock before eating. Has the ability to fly directly into the air from underwater. Depending on snowmelt, nesting usually starts in March or April. Dippers in lower elevations often nest a second time each season.

Eastern Kingbird
Tyrannus tyrannus

Size: 8" (20 cm)

Male: Mostly gray and black with a white chin and belly. Black head and tail with a distinct white band on the tip of the tail. Concealed red crown, rarely seen.

Female: same as male

Juvenile: same as adults

Nest: cup; male and female build; 1 brood per year

Eggs: 3–4; white with brown markings

Incubation: 16–18 days; female incubates

Fledging: 16–18 days; female and male feed the young

Migration: complete, to Mexico, Central America and South America

Food: insects, fruit

Compare: American Robin (p. 245) is larger and has a rust-red breast. Western Kingbird (p. 341) is yellow on the belly and under the wings. Look for the white band along the end of the tail to identify.

Stan's Notes: Found in open fields and prairies. Returns to the mating ground in spring, where pairs defend their territory. Seems to be unafraid of other birds and chases larger birds. Given the common name "King" for its bold attitude and behavior. In a hunting technique known as hawking, it perches on a branch and watches for insects, flies out to catch one, and then returns to the same perch. Becomes very vocal during late summer, when family members call back and forth to one another while hunting for insects. Fall migration begins in late August and early September, with groups of up to 20 individuals migrating together.

gray morph

brown morph

Western Screech-Owl

Megascops kennicottii

YEAR-ROUND

Size: 8–9" (20–23 cm); up to 1¾' wingspan

Male: A small, overall gray owl with bright-yellow eyes. Two short ear tufts. A short tail. Some birds are brownish.

Female: same as male

Juvenile: similar to adult of the same morph and lacks ear tufts

Nest: cavity, old woodpecker hole; 1 brood per year

Eggs: 2–6; white without markings

Incubation: 21–30 days; female incubates

Fledging: 25–30 days; male and female feed the young

Migration: non-migrator

Food: large insects, small mammals, birds

Compare: Western Screech-Owl is hard to confuse with its considerably larger cousin, the Great Horned Owl (p. 199).

Stan's Notes: The most common small owl in the state. An owl of suburban woodlands and backyards. Requires trees that are at least a foot in diameter for nesting and roosting, so it usually is found in older trees. A secondary cavity nester, which means it nests in tree cavities created by other birds. Usually not found in elevations above 4,000 feet (1,200 m). Densities in lower areas are about 1 bird per square mile (2.5 sq. km). Most screech-owls are gray; some are brown (see inset).

winter

breeding
p. 143

Dunlin
Calidris alpina

MIGRATION
WINTER

Size: 8–9" (20–23 cm)

Male: Winter adult has a brownish-gray back with a light-gray chest and white belly. Stout bill curves slightly downward at tip. Black legs.

Female: slightly larger than the male, with a longer bill

Juvenile: slightly rusty back with a spotty chest

Nest: ground; male and female construct; 1 brood per year

Eggs: 2–4; olive-buff or blue-green with red-brown markings

Incubation: 21–22 days; male incubates during the day, female incubates at night

Fledging: 19–21 days; male feeds the young, female often leaves before the young fledge

Migration: complete, to the coasts of the U.S., Mexico and Central America

Food: insects

Compare: Winter Dunlin has a stout down-turned bill and is overall gray.

Stan's Notes: Usually seen in gray winter plumage from August to early May. Breeding plumage is more commonly seen in the spring. Flights include heights of up to 100 feet (30 m) with brief gliding alternating with shallow flutters, and a rhythmic, repeating song. Huge flocks fly synchronously, with birds twisting and turning, flashing light and dark undersides. Males tend to fly farther south in winter than females. Doesn't nest in the state.

Townsend's Solitaire
Myadestes townsendi

YEAR-ROUND
SUMMER
WINTER

Size: 8½" (22 cm)

Male: All-gray robin look-alike. Prominent white ring around each eye. Wings slightly darker than the body. Long tail. Short dark bill. Dark legs.

Female: same as male

Juvenile: darker gray with a tan scaly appearance

Nest: cup; female builds; 1–2 broods per year

Eggs: 3–5; blue, green, gray or white with brown markings

Incubation: 12–14 days; female incubates

Fledging: 10–14 days; female and male feed young

Migration: partial to non-migrator; moves around in winter

Food: insects, fruit

Compare: American Robin (p. 245) has a red breast. Clark's Nutcracker (p. 251) has black wings. Canada Jay (p. 249) has a white head.

Stan's Notes: A summer resident of coniferous mountain forests, moving lower in winter. "Hawks" for insects, perching in trees and darting out to capture them. Eats berries in winter when insects are not available and actively defends a good berry source from other birds. Builds nest on ground sheltered by rocks or an overhang, or sometimes low in a tree or shrub. Song is a series of clear flute-like whistles without a distinct pattern. Shows white outer tail feathers and light tan patches on wings when in flight.

Gray Catbird
Dumetella carolinensis

SUMMER MIGRATION

Size: 9" (22.5 cm)

Male: Handsome slate-gray bird with a black crown and a long, thin, black bill. Often lifts up its tail, exposing a chestnut patch beneath.

Female: same as male

Juvenile: same as adults

Nest: cup; female and male build; 2 broods per year

Eggs: 4–6; blue-green without markings

Incubation: 12–13 days; female incubates

Fledging: 10–11 days; female and male feed young

Migration: complete, to Mexico and Central America

Food: insects, occasional fruit; visits suet feeders

Compare: The Eastern Kingbird (p. 235) is similar in size but has a white belly and a white band across its tail. To identify the Gray Catbird, look for the black crown and chestnut patch under the tail.

Stan's Notes: A secretive bird, more often heard than seen. The Chippewa Indians gave it a name that means "the bird that cries with grief" due to its raspy call. Called "Catbird" because the sound is like the meowing of a house cat. Often mimics other birds, rarely repeating the same phrases. Found in forest edges, backyards and parks. Builds its nest with small twigs. Nests in thick shrubs and quickly flies back into shrubs if approached. If a cowbird lays an egg in its nest, the catbird will quickly break it and eject it.

male

female

American Robin
Turdus migratorius

YEAR-ROUND

Size: 9–11" (23–28 cm)

Male: Familiar gray bird with a dark rust-red breast and a nearly black head and tail. White chin with black streaks. White eye-ring.

Female: similar to male, with a duller rust-red breast and a gray head

Juvenile: similar to female, with a speckled breast and brown back

Nest: cup; female builds with help from the male; 2–3 broods per year

Eggs: 4–7; pale blue without markings

Incubation: 12–14 days; female incubates

Fledging: 14–16 days; female and male feed the young

Migration: non-migrator in Washington; moves around to find food

Food: insects, fruit, berries, earthworms

Compare: Familiar bird to all. To differentiate the male from the female, compare the nearly black head and rust-red chest of the male with the gray head and duller chest of the female.

Stan's Notes: Although a complete migrator, it can be seen year-round throughout Washington. Can be heard singing all night long in spring. City robins sing louder than country robins in order to hear one another over traffic and noise. A robin isn't listening for worms when it turns its head to one side. It is focusing its sight out of one eye to look for dirt moving, which is caused by worms moving. Territorial, often fighting its reflection in a window. Males have dark heads and a brighter red breast than females.

male

female

California Quail
Callipepla californica

YEAR-ROUND

Size: 10" (25 cm)

Male: Plump gray quail with black face and chin. Prominent teardrop-shaped plume on the forehead. "Scaled" appearance on the belly, light brown to white. Pale-brown forehead.

Female: similar to male, lacks a black face and chin

Juvenile: similar to female

Nest: ground; female builds; 1 brood per year

Eggs: 12–16; white with brown markings

Incubation: 18–23 days; female incubates

Fledging: 8–10 days; female and male teach young to feed

Migration: non-migrator

Food: seeds, leaves, insects; visits ground feeders

Compare: Ring-necked Pheasant (p. 203) is larger and lacks the unique plume on the head of the Quail. More common than the Mountain Quail (not shown), which is brown and has an extremely long, thin plume on forehead. Look for plume on the forehead of both male and female to help identify the California Quail.

Stan's Notes: Prefers open fields, agricultural areas and sagebrush. Not found in dense forests or high elevations. Rarely flies, preferring to run away. Roosts in trees or dense shrubs at night, not on the ground. Usually seen in groups (coveys) of up to 100 individuals during winter, breaking up into small family units for breeding. Young stay with the family group until autumn. Has expanded its range in Washington over the past 70 years.

Canada Jay
Perisoreus canadensis

YEAR-ROUND

Size: 11½" (29 cm)

Male: Large gray bird with a white forehead and nape of neck. Short black bill. Dark eyes.

Female: same as male

Juvenile: sooty gray with a faint white whisker mark

Nest: cup; male and female construct; 1 brood per year

Eggs: 3–4; gray white, finely marked to unmarked

Incubation: 16–18 days; female incubates

Fledging: 14–15 days; male and female feed young

Migration: non-migrator

Food: insects, seeds, fruit, nuts; visits seed feeders

Compare: Steller's Jay (p. 87) and California Scrub-Jay (p. 89) are slightly smaller, and both have blue coloring. Clark's Nutcracker (p. 251) is slightly larger with black wings. Black-billed Magpie (p. 67) is nearly twice the size of Canada Jay, has a much longer tail and lacks the mostly white head.

Stan's Notes: A bird of coniferous woods in mid to high elevations. Called Camp Robber because it rummages through camps looking for scraps of food. Also known as Whisky Jack or Gray Jay. Easily tamed, it will fly to your hand if offered raisins or nuts. Will eat just about anything. Also stores extra food for winter, balling it together in a sticky mass, placing it on a tree limb, often concealing it with lichen or bark. Travels around in family units of 3–5, making good companions for campers, canoeists and high altitude hikers and climbers. Reminds some of an overgrown chickadee.

Clark's Nutcracker

Nucifraga columbiana

YEAR-ROUND

Size: 12" (30 cm)

Male: Gray with black wings and a narrow black band down the center of tail. Small white patches on long wings, seen in flight. Has a relatively short tail with a white undertail.

Female: same as male

Juvenile: same as adult

Nest: cup; female and male build; 1 brood a year

Eggs: 2–5; pale green with brown markings

Incubation: 16–18 days; female incubates

Fledging: 14–15 days; male and female feed young

Migration: non-migrator

Food: seeds, insects, berries, eggs, mammals

Compare: The Steller's Jay (p. 87) is dark blue with a black crest. Canada Jay (p. 249) is slightly smaller and lacks the Nutcracker's black wings. Look for the Clark's Nutcracker's white wing patches to identify it.

Stan's Notes: A high-country bird found in coniferous forests. It has a varied diet but relies heavily on pinyon seeds, frequently caching large amounts to consume later or feed to young. Has a large pouch in its throat (sublingual pouch), which it uses to transport seeds. Studies show the birds can carry up to 100 seeds at a time. Nests early in the year, often while snow still covers the ground, relying on stored foods. A "Lewis and Clark" bird, first recorded by William Clark in 1805 in Idaho.

soaring

juvenile

Sharp-shinned Hawk

Accipiter striatus

YEAR-ROUND
WINTER

Size: 10–14" (25–36 cm); up to 2' wingspan

Male: Small woodland hawk with a gray back and head and a rust-red chest. Short wings. Long, squared tail and several dark tail bands, with the widest at the end of the tail. Red eyes.

Female: same as male but larger

Juvenile: same size as adults, with a brown back, heavy streaking on the chest and yellow eyes

Nest: platform; female builds; 1 brood per year

Eggs: 4–5; white with brown markings

Incubation: 32–35 days; female incubates

Fledging: 24–27 days; female and male feed the young

Migration: non-migrator to partial, to southern states, Mexico and Central America

Food: birds, small mammals

Compare: Cooper's Hawk (p. 259) is larger and has a larger head, a slightly longer neck and a rounded tail. Look for the squared tail to help identify the Sharp-shinned Hawk.

Stan's Notes: A hawk of backyards, parks and woodlands. Seen swooping on birds visiting feeders and chasing them as they flee. Its short wingspan and long tail help it to maneuver through thick stands of trees in pursuit of prey. Calls a loud, high-pitched "kik-kik-kik-kik." Named "Sharp-shinned" for the sharp projection (keel) on the leading edge of its shin. A bird's shin is actually below the ankle (rather than above it, like ours) on the tarsus bone of its foot. In most birds, the tarsus bone is rounded, not sharp.

YEAR-ROUND

Rock Pigeon
Columba livia

Size: 13" (33 cm)

Male: No set color pattern. Shades of gray to white with patches of gleaming, iridescent green and blue. Often has a light rump patch.

Female: same as male

Juvenile: same as adults

Nest: platform; female builds; 3–4 broods per year

Eggs: 1–2; white without markings

Incubation: 18–20 days; female and male incubate

Fledging: 25–26 days; female and male feed the young

Migration: non-migrator

Food: seeds

Compare: The larger Band-tailed Pigeon (p. 257) is uniformly colored and patterned and has a disproportionately long tail. The Mourning Dove (p. 159) is smaller and light brown and lacks the variety of color combinations of the Rock Pigeon.

Stan's Notes: Also known as the Domestic Pigeon. Formerly known as the Rock Dove. Introduced to North America from Europe by the early settlers. Most common around cities and barnyards, where it scratches for seeds. One of the few birds with a wide variety of colors, produced by years of selective breeding while in captivity. Parents feed the young a regurgitated liquid known as crop-milk for the first few days of life. One of the few birds that can drink without tilting its head back. Nests under bridges or on buildings, balconies, barns and sheds. Was once thought to be a nuisance in cities and was poisoned. Now, many cities have Peregrine Falcons (p. 261) feeding on Rock Pigeons, which keeps their numbers in check.

Band-tailed Pigeon

Patagioenas fasciata

YEAR-ROUND

Size: 14½" (37 cm)

Male: A typical pigeon-shaped body. Overall gray with a narrow white band on nape of neck. Dark eyes. Black-tipped yellow bill. Yellow legs. Disproportionately long tail.

Female: same as male

Juvenile: similar to adult, lacks white band on neck

Nest: cup; female and male construct; 2–3 broods per year

Eggs: 1–2; white without markings

Incubation: 18–20 days; female and male incubate

Fledging: 25–27 days; female and male feed young

Migration: non-migrator

Food: nuts, seeds, fruit, berries

Compare: The smaller Rock Pigeon (p. 255) comes in a wide variety of colors and patterns, unlike the uniformly colored and patterned Band-tailed. Look for a long tail and the uniform color of Band-taileds in a flock.

Stan's Notes: A common pigeon in the western half of the state. Prefers residential areas and city parks with suitable large conifer trees, in low to middle elevations. Has a nomadic lifestyle. Moves around constantly in response to the food supply. Often seen flying in groups. Male performs a courtship flight of rapid flapping alternating with short glides, then landing and bowing to female. Nests in scattered pairs. Easily distinguished from the Rock Pigeon by its uniform gray color and long tail.

soaring

juvenile

Cooper's Hawk
Accipiter cooperii

YEAR-ROUND

Size: 14–20" (36–51 cm); up to 3' wingspan

Male: Medium-size hawk with short wings and a long, rounded tail with several black bands. Slate-gray back, rusty breast, dark wing tips. Gray bill with a bright-yellow spot at the base. Dark-red eyes.

Female: similar to male but larger

Juvenile: brown back, brown streaking on the breast, bright-yellow eyes

Nest: platform; male and female construct; 1 brood per year

Eggs: 2–4; greenish with brown markings

Incubation: 32–36 days; female and male incubate

Fledging: 28–32 days; male and female feed the young

Migration: Non-migrator to partial migrator; moves around to find food in winter; many move out of the state in winter

Food: small birds, mammals

Compare: Sharp-shinned Hawk (p. 253) is much smaller, lighter gray and has a squared tail. Look for the banded, rounded tail to help identify Cooper's Hawk.

Stan's Notes: Found in many habitats, from woodlands to parks and backyards. Stubby wings help it to navigate around trees while it chases small birds. Will ambush prey, flying into heavy brush or even running on the ground. Comes to feeders, hunting for birds. Flies with long glides followed by a few quick flaps. Calls a loud, clear "cack-cack-cack-cack." The young have gray eyes that turn bright yellow at 1 year and turn dark red later, after 3–5 years.

juvenile

in-flight
juvenile

in flight

Peregrine Falcon

Falco peregrinus

SUMMER
MIGRATION
WINTER

Size: 16–20" (41–51 cm); up to 3¾' wingspan

Male: Dark-gray back and tan-to-white chest. Horizontal bars on belly, legs and undertail. Dark "hood" head marking and wide black mustache. Yellow base of bill and eye-ring. Yellow legs.

Female: similar to male but noticeably larger

Juvenile: overall darker than adults, with heavy streaking on the chest and belly

Nest: ground (scrape) on a cliff edge, tall building, bridge or smokestack; 1 brood per year

Eggs: 3–4; white, some with brown markings

Incubation: 29–32 days; female and male incubate

Fledging: 35–42 days; male and female feed the young

Migration: partial to complete migrator; some remain in Washington in winter

Food: birds (Rock Pigeons in cities, shorebirds and waterfowl in rural areas)

Compare: The American Kestrel (p. 153) is smaller and has 2 vertical black stripes on its face. Look for the dark "hood" head marking and mustache marks to identify the Peregrine Falcon.

Stan's Notes: A wide-bodied raptor that hunts many bird species. Lives in many cities, diving (stooping) on pigeons at speeds of up to 200 miles (322 km) per hour, which knocks them to the ground. Soars with its wings flat, often riding thermals. During courtship, the male brings food to the female and performs aerial displays. Likes to nest on a high ledge or platform for a good view of its territory. A solitary nester and monogamous.

female
p. 189

male

soaring

Northern Harrier
Circus hudsonius

YEAR-ROUND
SUMMER

Size: 18–22" (45–56 cm); up to 4' wingspan

Male: Slender, low-flying hawk. Silver-gray with a large white rump patch and white belly. Long tail with faint narrow bands. Black wing tips. Yellow eyes.

Female: dark-brown back, brown streaking on breast and belly, large white rump patch, thin black tail bands, black wing tips, yellow eyes

Juvenile: similar to female, with an orange breast

Nest: ground; female and male construct; 1 brood per year

Eggs: 4–8; bluish white without markings

Incubation: 31–32 days; female incubates

Fledging: 30–35 days; male and female feed the young

Migration: non-migrator to partial migrator

Food: mice, snakes, insects, small birds

Compare: Slimmer than the Red-tailed Hawk (p. 195). Cooper's Hawk (p. 259) has a rusty breast. Look for a low-gliding hawk with a large white rump patch to identify the male Harrier.

Stan's Notes: One of the easiest of hawks to identify. Glides just above the ground, following the contours of the land while searching for prey. Holds its wings just above horizontal, tilting back and forth in the wind, similar to Turkey Vultures. Formerly called the Marsh Hawk due to its habit of hunting over marshes. Feeds and nests on the ground. Will also preen and rest on the ground. Unlike other hawks, mainly uses its hearing to find prey, followed by sight. At any age, has a distinctive owl-like face disk.

female
p. 185

male

Gadwall
Mareca strepera

YEAR-ROUND

Size: 19" (48 cm)

Male: A plump gray duck with a brown head and a distinctive black rump. White belly. Chestnut-tinged wings. Bright-white wing linings. Small white wing patch, seen when swimming. Gray bill.

Female: similar to female Mallard, a mottled brown with a pronounced color change from dark-brown body to light-brown neck and head, bright-white wing linings, small white wing patch, gray bill with orange sides

Juvenile: similar to female

Nest: ground; female lines the nest with fine grass and down feathers plucked from her chest; 1 brood per year

Eggs: 8–11; white without markings

Incubation: 24–27 days; female incubates

Fledging: 48–56 days; young feed themselves

Migration: non-migrator; moves around to find food

Food: aquatic insects

Compare: Male Gadwall is one of the few gray ducks. Look for its distinctive black rump.

Stan's Notes: A duck of shallow marshes with lots of vegetation. Found in freshwater wetlands in eastern Washington, but is most common in the urban and suburban areas of western Washington, especially in southern parts of Puget Sound. Consumes mostly plant material, dunking its head in water to feed rather than tipping forward, like other dabbling ducks. Nests within 300 feet (90 m) of water. Establishes pair bond in winter.

265

in flight

Canada Goose
Branta canadensis

YEAR-ROUND

Size: 25–43" (64–109 cm); up to 5½' wingspan

Male: Large gray goose with a black neck and head. White chin and cheek strap.

Female: same as male

Juvenile: same as adults

Nest: platform, on the ground; female builds; 1 brood per year

Eggs: 5–10; white without markings

Incubation: 25–30 days; female incubates

Fledging: 42–55 days; male and female teach the young to feed

Migration: non-migrator to partial migrator; will move to any place with open water

Food: aquatic plants, insects, seeds

Compare: Large goose that is rarely confused with any other bird.

Stan's Notes: Common year-round resident throughout the state. Calls a classic "honk-honk-honk," especially in flight. Flocks fly in a large V when traveling long distances. Begins breeding in the third year. Adults mate for many years. If threatened, they will hiss as a warning. Males stand as sentinels at the edge of their group and will bob their heads and become aggressive if approached. Adults molt their primary flight feathers while raising their young, rendering family groups temporarily flightless. Several subspecies vary in the U.S. Generally eastern groups are paler than western. Their size also varies, decreasing northward. The smallest subspecies is in the Arctic.

in flight

Great Blue Heron

Ardea herodias

Size: 42–48" (107–122 cm); up to 6' wingspan

Male: Tall and gray. Black eyebrows end in long plumes at the back of the head. Long yellow bill. Long feathers at the base of the neck drop down in a kind of necklace. Long legs.

Female: same as male

Juvenile: same as adults, but more brown than gray, with a black crown; lacks plumes

Nest: platform in a colony; male and female build; 1 brood per year

Eggs: 3–5; blue-green without markings

Incubation: 27–28 days; female and male incubate

Fledging: 56–60 days; male and female feed the young

Migration: non-migrator to partial migrator; moves around find open water and food in winter; many move out of the state in winter

Food: small fish, frogs, insects, snakes, baby birds

Compare: The Sandhill Crane (p. 271) has a red cap. Look for the long, yellow bill to help identify the Great Blue Heron.

Stan's Notes: One of the most common herons. Found in open water, from small ponds to large lakes. Stalks small fish in shallow water. Will strike at mice, squirrels and nearly anything it comes across. Red-winged Blackbirds will attack it to stop it from taking their babies out of the nest. In flight, it holds its neck in an S shape and slightly cups its wings, while the legs trail straight out behind. Nests in a colony of up to 100 birds. Nests in trees near or hanging over water. Barks like a dog when startled.

in flight

in-flight
rusty stain

rusty
stain

Sandhill Crane
Grus canadensis

YEAR-ROUND
MIGRATION

Size: 42–48" (107–122 cm); up to 7' wingspan

Male: Elegant gray crane with long legs and neck. Wings and body often rust brown from mud staining. Scarlet-red cap. Yellow to red eyes.

Female: same as male

Juvenile: dull brown with yellow eyes; lacks a red cap

Nest: ground; female and male construct; 1 brood per year

Eggs: 2; olive with brown markings

Incubation: 28–32 days; female and male incubate

Fledging: 65 days; female and male feed the young

Migration: non-migrator to partial, to southern states and Mexico

Food: insects, fruit, worms, plants, amphibians

Compare: Great Blue Heron (p. 269) has a longer bill and holds its neck in an S shape during flight. Look for the scarlet-red cap to help identify the Sandhill Crane.

Stan's Notes: Preens mud into its feathers, staining its plumage rust brown (see insets). Gives a very loud and distinctive rattling call, often heard before the bird is seen. Flight is characteristic, with a faster upstroke, making the wings look like they're flicking in flight. Can fly at heights of over 10,000 feet (3,050 m). Nests on the ground in a large mound of aquatic vegetation. Performs a spectacular mating dance: The birds will face each other, then bow and jump into the air while making loud cackling sounds and flapping their wings. They will also flip sticks and grass into the air during their dance.

male

female

Calliope Hummingbird
Selasphorus calliope

SUMMER

Size: 3¼" (8 cm)

Male: Iridescent green head, back and tail. Breast and belly white to tan. V-shaped iridescent rosy red throat patch (gorget). A very short, thin bill and short tail compared with other hummingbirds. Wing tips reach to tip of tail.

Female: same as male, but thin, spotty throat patch

Juvenile: similar to female

Nest: cup; female builds; 1 brood per year

Eggs: 1–2; white without markings

Incubation: 15–17 days; female incubates

Fledging: 18–22 days; female feeds the young

Migration: complete, to Central and South America

Food: nectar, insects; will come to nectar feeders

Compare: Smaller than other hummingbirds. Look for a short thin bill, short tail and wing tips extending past the tail when perched. Female is similar to female Anna's Hummingbird (p. 275) and Rufous Hummingbird (p. 289), but it has a shorter, thinner bill and short tail.

Stan's Notes: The smallest bird in North America. Common in open forest and brushy areas in lower elevations of eastern Washington. A relatively quiet bird that will come to nectar feeders. During the breeding season, males can be heard zinging around while displaying for females. Females are hard to distinguish from other female hummingbirds. Often builds nest on branches of pine trees. Juvenile males obtain a partial throat patch by fall of their first year.

male

female

Anna's Hummingbird
Calypte anna

YEAR-ROUND

Size: 4" (10 cm)

Male: Iridescent green body with dark head, chin and neck. In direct sunlight, the dark head shines a deep rose-red. Breast and belly are dull gray. White eye-ring.

Female: similar to male, but head reflects only a few red flecks instead of a complete rose-red

Juvenile: similar to female

Nest: cup; female builds; 2–3 broods per year

Eggs: 1–3; white without markings

Incubation: 14–19 days; female incubates

Fledging: 18–23 days; female feeds the young

Migration: partial migrator to non-migrator; many move to the coast of southern California and Mexico

Food: nectar, insects; will come to nectar feeders

Compare: Rufous Hummingbird (p. 289) is slightly smaller and has a characteristic burnt-orange color.

Stan's Notes: Common western coastal hummingbird found from Baja, California, to British Columbia. Unknown in the state before the late 1950s, it has since expanded northward and is now considered common along the coast. An early nester. Female builds a tiny nest on chaparral-covered hillsides and in canyons. Feathers on head are black until seen in direct sun. Reflected sunlight turns the male's head bright rosy red. Apparently consumes more insects than other species of hummingbirds.

male

female

Violet-green Swallow
Tachycineta thalassina

SUMMER

Size: 5¼" (13.5 cm)

Male: Dull emerald green crown, nape and back. Violet-blue wings and tail. White chest and belly. White cheeks with white extending above the eyes. Wings extend beyond the tail when perching.

Female: same as male, only duller

Juvenile: similar to adult of the same sex

Nest: cavity; female and male build nest in tree cavities, old woodpecker holes; 1 brood per year

Eggs: 4–6; pale white with brown markings

Incubation: 13–14 days; female incubates

Fledging: 18–24 days; female and male feed the young

Migration: complete, to Central and South America

Food: insects

Compare: Similar size as the Cliff Swallow (p. 113) which has a distinctive tan-to-rust pattern on the head. Barn Swallow (p. 81) has a distinctive, deeply forked tail. The Tree Swallow (p. 79) is mostly deep blue, lacking any emerald green of the Violet-green Swallow.

Stan's Notes: Commonly seen throughout Washington. A solitary nester in tree cavities and rarely beneath cliff overhangs. Like Tree Swallows, it can be attracted with a nest box. Will search for miles for errant feathers to line its nest. Tail is short and wing tips extend beyond the end of it, seen when perching. Returns to the state in late April and begins nesting in May. Young often leave the nest by June. On cloudy days they look black but on sunny days they look metallic green.

in flight

Green Heron
Butorides virescens

SUMMER

Size: 16–22" (41–56 cm)

Male: Short and stocky. Blue-green back and rust-red neck and breast. Dark-green crest. Short legs are normally yellow but turn bright orange during the breeding season.

Female: same as male

Juvenile: similar to adults, with a bluish-gray back and white-streaked breast and neck

Nest: platform; female and male build; 2 broods per year

Eggs: 2–4; light green without markings

Incubation: 21–25 days; female and male incubate

Fledging: 35–36 days; female and male feed the young

Migration: complete migrator, to California, Arizona and Mexico

Food: small fish, aquatic insects, small amphibians

Compare: Great Blue Heron (p. 269) is larger. Green Heron lacks the long neck of other herons. Look for a small heron with a dark-green back and crest to identify the Green.

Stan's Notes: Often gives an explosive, rasping "skyew" call when startled. Holds its head close to its body, which sometimes makes it look like it doesn't have a neck. Waits on the shore or wades stealthily, hunting for small fish, aquatic insects and small amphibians. Places an object, such as an insect, on the water's surface to attract fish to catch. Nests in a tall tree, often a short distance from the water. The nest can be very high up in the tree. Babies give a loud ticking sound, like the ticktock of a clock.

female
p. 177

male

Wood Duck
Aix sponsa

YEAR-ROUND SUMMER

Size: 17–20" (43–51 cm)

Male: Small, highly ornamented dabbling duck. Mostly green head and crest patterned with black and white. Rusty chest and a white belly. Red eyes.

Female: brown duck with a bright-white eye-ring, not-so-obvious crest and blue patch on wings (speculum), often hidden

Juvenile: similar to female

Nest: cavity; female lines an old woodpecker cavity or a nest box in a tree; 1 brood per year

Eggs: 10–15; creamy white without markings

Incubation: 28–36 days; female incubates

Fledging: 56–68 days; female teaches the young to feed

Migration: complete, to southwestern states; partial to non-migrator in parts of Washington

Food: aquatic insects, plants, seeds

Compare: Male Northern Shoveler (p. 285) is larger with a long wide bill. Male Green-winged Teal (p. 165) lacks Wood Duck's showy colors.

Stan's Notes: A duck of quiet, shallow backwater ponds. Nearly extinct around 1900 due to overhunting, doing well now. Nests in tree cavity or nest box. Seen flying in forests or perching on high branches. Female takes off with a loud squealing call and enters the nest cavity from full flight. Lays some eggs in a neighboring nest (egg dumping), resulting in more than 20 eggs in some clutches. Hatchlings stay in nest for 24 hours, then jump from as high as 60 feet (18 m) to the ground or water to follow their mother. They never return to the nest.

female
p. 183

male

Mallard
Anas platyrhynchos

YEAR-ROUND

Size: 19–21" (48–53 cm)

Male: Large, bulbous green head, white necklace and rust-brown or chestnut chest. Gray-and-white sides. Yellow bill. Orange legs and feet.

Female: brown with an orange-and-black bill and blue-and-white wing mark (speculum)

Juvenile: same as female but with a yellow bill

Nest: ground; female builds; 1 brood per year

Eggs: 7–10; greenish to whitish, unmarked

Incubation: 26–30 days; female incubates

Fledging: 42–52 days; female leads the young to food

Migration: partial to non-migrator in Washington

Food: seeds, plants, aquatic insects; will come to ground feeders offering corn

Compare: Male Northern Shoveler (p. 285) has a white chest with rusty sides and a very large, spoon-shaped bill. Male Gadwall (p. 265) lacks the male Mallard's green head. Look for the green head and yellow bill to identify the male Mallard.

Stan's Notes: A familiar dabbling duck of lakes and ponds. Also found in rivers, streams and some backyards. Tips forward to feed on vegetation on the bottom of shallow water. The name "Mallard" comes from the Latin word *masculus*, meaning "male," referring to the male's habit of taking no part in raising the young. Male and female have white underwings and white tails, but only the male has black central tail feathers that curl upward. Unlike the female, the male doesn't quack. Returns to its birthplace each year.

female
p. 181

male

Northern Shoveler
Anas clypeata

Size: 19–21" (48–53 cm)

Male: Medium-sized duck with an iridescent green head, rust sides, white chest. Extraordinarily large, spoon-shaped bill, almost always held pointed toward the water.

Female: brown and black all over, green wing patch (speculum) and a large spoon-shaped bill

Juvenile: same as female

Nest: ground; female builds; 1 brood per year

Eggs: 9–12; olive without markings

Incubation: 22–25 days; female incubates

Fledging: 30–60 days; female leads the young to food

Migration: non-migrator to partial migrator, to southwestern states, Mexico and Central America

Food: aquatic insects, plants

Compare: Male Mallard (p. 283) is similar, but it lacks the large spoon-shaped bill. The male Wood Duck (p. 281) is smaller and has a crest. Male Cinnamon Teal (p. 169) also has cinnamon-colored sides, but it is smaller and has a cinnamon-colored head.

Stan's Notes: One of several species of shovelers. Called "Shoveler" due to the peculiar, shovel-like shape of its bill. Given the common name "Northern" because it is the only species of these ducks in North America. Seen in shallow wetlands, ponds and small lakes in flocks of 5–10 birds. Flocks fly in tight formation. Swims low in water, pointing its large bill toward the water as if it's too heavy to lift. Feeds mainly by filtering tiny aquatic insects and plants from the surface of the water with its bill.

in flight

female
p. 305

male

Common Merganser
Mergus merganser

YEAR-ROUND

Size: 26–28" (66–71 cm)

Male: Long, thin, duck-like bird with a green head and black back. White sides, chest and neck. Long, pointed, orange bill. Often looks black and white in poor light.

Female: same size and shape as the male, with a rust-red head and ragged "hair," gray body, white chest and chin

Juvenile: same as female

Nest: cavity; female lines an old woodpecker hole or a natural cavity; 1 brood per year

Eggs: 9–11; ivory without markings

Incubation: 28–33 days; female incubates

Fledging: 70–80 days; female feeds the young

Migration: partial to non-migrator in Washington

Food: small fish, aquatic insects, amphibians

Compare: The male Mallard (p. 283) is smaller and lacks the black back and long, pointed, orange bill.

Stan's Notes: Seen on any open water during the winter but more common along large rivers than lakes. A large, shallow-water diver that feeds on fish in 10–15 feet (3–4.5 m) of water. Bill has a fine, serrated-like edge that helps catch slippery fish. Female often lays some eggs in other merganser nests (egg dumping), resulting in up to 15 young in some broods. Male leaves female once she starts incubating. Orphans are accepted by other merganser mothers with young. Fast flight, often low and close to the water, in groups but not in formation. Usually not vocal except for an alarm call.

male

female

Rufous Hummingbird
Selasphorus rufus

Size: 3¾" (9.5 cm)

Male: Tiny burnt-orange bird with a black throat patch (gorget) that reflects orange-red in sunlight. White chest. Green-to-tan flanks.

Female: same as male, but lacking the throat patch

Juvenile: similar to female

Nest: cup; female builds; 1–2 broods per year

Eggs: 1–3; white without markings

Incubation: 14–17 days; female incubates

Fledging: 21–26 days; female feeds young

Migration: complete, to Central and South America

Food: nectar, insects; will come to nectar feeders

Compare: Identify it by the unique orange-red (rufous) color.

Stan's Notes: One of the smallest birds in the state. This is a bold, hardy hummer. Frequently seen well out of its normal range in the western U.S., showing up along the East Coast. Visits hummingbird feeders in your yard during migration. Does not sing, but it will chatter or buzz to communicate. Weighing just 2–3 grams, it takes about five average-sized hummingbirds to equal the weight of one chickadee. The heart beats up to an incredible 1,260 times per minute. Male performs a spectacular pendulum-like flight over the perched female. After mating, the female will fly off to build a nest and raise young, without any help from her mate. Constructs a soft, flexible nest that expands to accommodate the growing young.

female
p. 337

male

Bullock's Oriole
Icterus bullockii

SUMMER

Size: 8" (20 cm)

Male: Bright-orange-and-black bird. Black crown, eye line, nape, chin, back and wings with a bold white patch on wings.

Female: dull-yellow overall, pale-white belly, white wing bars on gray-to-black wings

Juvenile: similar to female

Nest: pendulous; female and male build; 1 brood per year

Eggs: 4–6; pale white to gray, brown markings

Incubation: 12–14 days; female incubates

Fledging: 12–14 days; female and male feed young

Migration: complete, to Central and South America

Food: insects, berries, nectar; visits nectar feeders

Compare: Look for Bullock's bright markings and a thin black line running through each eye.

Stan's Notes: So closely related to Baltimore Orioles of the eastern U.S., at one time both were considered a single species. Interbreeds with Baltimores where their ranges overlap. Most common in the state where cottonwood trees grow along rivers and other wetlands. Also found at edges of clearings, in city parks, on farms and along irrigation ditches. Hanging sock-like nest is constructed of plant fibers such as inner bark of junipers and willows. Will incorporate yarn and thread into its nest if offered at the time of nest building.

female
p. 139

male

Black-headed Grosbeak

Pheucticus melanocephalus

SUMMER

Size: 8" (20 cm)

Male: Stocky bird with burnt-orange chest, neck and rump. Black head, tail and wings. Irregularly shaped white wing patches. Large bill, with upper bill darker than lower.

Female: appears like an overgrown sparrow, overall brown with a lighter breast and belly, large two-toned bill, prominent white eyebrows, yellow wing linings, as seen in flight

Juvenile: similar to adult of the same sex

Nest: cup; female builds; 1 brood per year

Eggs: 3–4; pale green or bluish, brown markings

Incubation: 11–13 days; female and male incubate

Fledging: 11–13 days; female and male feed young

Migration: complete, to Mexico, Central America and South America

Food: seeds, insects, fruit; comes to seed feeders

Compare: The male Bullock's Oriole (p. 291) has more white on wings than the male Black-headed. Same size as the male Evening Grosbeak (p. 339), but male Black-headed has an orange breast and lacks a yellow belly. Look for Black-headed's large bicolored bill.

Stan's Notes: A cosmopolitan bird that nests in a wide variety of habitats. Both the male and female sing and will aggressively defend the nest against intruders. Song is very similar to American Robin's (p. 245) and Western Tanager's (p. 335), making it hard to tell them apart by song. Populations increasing in Washington and across the U.S.

male

female

Varied Thrush

Ixoreus naevius

YEAR-ROUND
SUMMER
WINTER

Size: 9½" (24 cm)

Male: Potbellied robin-like bird with orange eyebrows, chin, breast and wing bars. Head, neck and back are gray to blue. Black breast band and eye mark.

Female: browner version of male, lacking the black breast band

Juvenile: similar to female

Nest: cup; female builds; 1–2 broods per year

Eggs: 3–5; pale blue with brown markings

Incubation: 12–14 days; female and male incubate

Fledging: 10–15 days; female and male feed young

Migration: partial migrator to non-migrator, to West Coast states

Food: insects, fruit

Compare: Similar size and shape as American Robin (p. 245), but the Varied Thrush has a warm-orange breast unlike the red breast of Robin. Male Thrush has a distinctive black breast band.

Stan's Notes: An intriguing-looking bird. Nests in Alaska, Canada and the mountains of Washington and Oregon. Prefers moist coniferous forests. It is most common in dense, older coniferous forests in high elevations. Moves to lower elevations in the winter, where it is often seen in towns, orchards or thickets, or migrates to California. Seen during winter in flocks of up to 20 birds. Individual Varied Thrush birds sometimes fly eastward in winter, and they can show up in nearly any state before returning to the West Coast for breeding.

male

female
p. 101

yellow
male

House Finch
Huemorhous mexicanus

YEAR-ROUND

Size: 5" (13 cm)

Male: Small finch with a red-to-orange face, throat, chest and rump. Brown cap. Brown marking behind eyes. White belly with brown streaks. Brown wings with white streaks.

Female: brown with a heavily streaked white chest

Juvenile: similar to female

Nest: cup, sometimes in cavities; female builds; 2 broods per year

Eggs: 4–5; pale blue, lightly marked

Incubation: 12–14 days; female incubates

Fledging: 15–19 days; female and male feed the young

Migration: non-migrator to partial migrator; moves around to find food

Food: seeds, fruit, leaf buds; visits seed feeders and feeders that offer grape jelly

Compare: Male Cassin's Finch (p. 301) is similar, but it is rosy red, unlike the orange-red of male House Finch, and it lacks a brown cap. Look for the streaked chest and belly and the brown cap to help identify the male House Finch.

Stan's Notes: Can be a common bird at your feeders. Very social, visiting feeders in small flocks. Likes to nest in hanging flower baskets. Male sings a loud, cheerful warbling song. Historically it occurred from the Pacific Coast to the Rockies, with only a few reaching the eastern side. House Finches that were originally introduced to Long Island, New York, from the western U.S. in the 1940s have since populated the entire eastern U.S. Suffers from a disease that causes the eyes to crust, resulting in blindness and death.

female
p. 117

male

Purple Finch
Haemorhous purpureus

YEAR-ROUND

Size: 6" (15 cm)

Male: Raspberry-red head, cap, chest, back and rump. Brownish wings and tail. Large bill.

Female: heavily streaked brown-and-white bird with bold white eyebrows

Juvenile: same as female

Nest: cup; female and male build; 1 brood per year

Eggs: 4–5; greenish blue with brown markings

Incubation: 12–13 days; female incubates

Fledging: 13–14 days; female and male feed the young

Migration: non-migrator to irruptive; moves around in search of food

Food: seeds, insects, fruit; comes to seed feeders

Compare: Male House Finch (p. 297) is orange-red with a streaked breast and a brown cap. Male Red Crossbill (p. 303) is similar, but it has a unique long, crossed bill. Look for the raspberry cap to help identify the male Purple Finch.

Stan's Notes: A year-round resident, common in non-residential areas. Prefers open woods or woodland edges of low to middle elevation conifer forest. Feeds mainly on seeds; ash tree seeds are an important source of food. Travels in flocks of up to 50 birds. Visits seed feeders along with House Finches, which makes it hard to tell them apart. Flies in the typical undulating, up-and-down pattern of finches. Sings a rich, loud song. Gives a distinctive "tic" note only in flight. The male is not purple. The Latin species name *purpureus* means "purple" (and other reddish colors).

female
p. 123

male

Cassin's Finch

Haemorhous cassinii

YEAR-ROUND
SUMMER

Size: 6½" (16 cm)

Male: Overall light wash of crimson red with an especially bright-red crown. Distinct brown streaks on back and wings. White belly.

Female: overall brown to gray, fine black streaks on the back and wings, heavily streaked white chest and belly

Juvenile: similar to female

Nest: cup; female builds; 1–2 broods per year

Eggs: 3–5; white without markings

Incubation: 12–14 days; female incubates

Fledging: 14–18 days; female and male feed young

Migration: partial migrator to non-migrator; will move around to find food

Food: seeds, insects, fruits, berries; will visit seed feeders

Compare: Male House Finch (p. 297) has a brown cap, is heavily streaked on its flanks and is orange-red. Gray-crowned Rosy-Finch (p. 119) is similar, but Cassin's Finch is much more red.

Stan's Notes: This is a common mountain finch of eastern Washington's coniferous forests. Usually forages for seeds on the ground, but eats evergreen buds and aspen and willow catkins. Breeds in May. A colony nester, depending on the regional source of food. The more food available, the larger the colony. Male sings a rapid warble, often imitating other birds such as jays, tanagers and grosbeaks. A cowbird host.

female
p. 333

male

Red Crossbill
Loxia curvirostra

YEAR-ROUND
WINTER

Size: 6½" (16 cm)

Male: Sparrow-sized bird, dirty-red to orange with bright-red crown and rump. Long, pointed, crossed bill. Dark-brown wings and a short dark-brown tail.

Female: pale-yellow chest, light-gray throat patch, a crossed bill, dark-brown wings and tail

Juvenile: streaked with tinges of yellow, bill gradually crosses about 2 weeks after fledging

Nest: cup; female builds; 1 brood per year

Eggs: 3–4; bluish white with brown markings

Incubation: 14–18 days; female incubates

Fledging: 16–20 days; female and male feed young

Migration: non-migrator to irruptive, moves around the state in winter to find food.

Food: seeds, leaf buds; comes to seed feeders

Compare: Male House Finch (p. 297) is smaller and lacks the dark-brown wings. Look for the unique crossed bill to help identify.

Stan's Notes: The long crossed bill is adapted for extracting seeds from pine and spruce cones, its favorite food. Often dangles upside down like a parrot to reach cones. Also seen on the ground where it eats grit, which helps digest food. Nests in coniferous forests at any elevation, mainly west of the Cascades. Plumage can be highly variable among individuals. While it is a resident nester. migrating crossbills from farther north move into the state during winter, searching for food, swelling populations. This irruptive behavior makes it more common in some winters and nonexistent in others.

in flight

male
p. 287

female

Common Merganser

Mergus merganser

YEAR-ROUND

Size: 26–28" (66–71 cm)

Female: Long, thin, duck-like bird with a rust-red head and ragged "hair." Gray body and white chest and chin. Long, pointed, orange bill.

Male: same size and shape as the female, but with a green head, a black back and white sides

Juvenile: same as female

Nest: cavity; female lines an old woodpecker hole or a natural cavity; 1 brood per year

Eggs: 9–11; ivory without markings

Incubation: 28–33 days; female incubates

Fledging: 70–80 days; female feeds the young

Migration: partial to non-migrator in Washington

Food: small fish, aquatic insects

Compare: Hard to confuse with other birds. Look for a rust-red head with ragged "hair," a white chin and a long, pointed, orange bill to identify.

Stan's Notes: Seen on any open water during the winter but more common along large rivers than lakes. A large, shallow-water diver that feeds on fish in 10–15 feet (3–4.5 m) of water. Bill has a fine, serrated-like edge that helps catch slippery fish. The female often lays some eggs in other merganser nests (egg dumping), resulting in up to 15 young in some broods. Male leaves the female once she starts incubating. Orphans are accepted by other merganser mothers with young. Fast flight, often low and close to the water, in groups but not in formation. Usually not vocal except for an alarm call that sounds like a muffled quack.

in flight

breeding

winter

Mew Gull
Larus canus

WINTER

Size: 16" (40 cm); up to 3½' wingspan

Male: White gull with dark-gray back and wings. Black wing tips. Red ring around dark eyes. Yellow legs. Breeding has a small unmarked yellow bill. Winter plumage has a brown-streaked head and neck. Yellow bill with a dark ring around the tip.

Female: same as male

Juvenile: gray to brown overall with a black-tipped yellow bill

Nest: ground; female and male construct; 1 brood per year

Eggs: 2–3; brown with brown markings

Incubation: 24–26 days; female and male incubate

Fledging: 30–32 days; female and male feed young

Migration: complete, to western coastal U.S. and Mexico

Food: insects, fish, shellfish, fruit

Compare: Herring Gull (p. 315) and Glaucous-winged Gull (p. 317) are much larger. Look for the tiny yellow bill and diminutive size.

Stan's Notes: Small gull with a remarkably small bill. A common winter visitor, often seen with other gulls. Often drops sea urchins from heights to crack open and eat. This is a three-year gull, taking three years to reach maturity. Starts out entirely light brown. With a brown-streaked head and neck, the second-year gull resembles the winter adult. Third-year gull has breeding plumage. Doesn't nest in the state, nesting in northwestern Canada and Alaska instead. The young return to their natal colony to nest. Known in Europe as Common Gull.

in flight

breeding

juvenile

winter

Ring-billed Gull
Larus delawarensis

YEAR-ROUND
SUMMER
WINTER

Size: 18–20" (45–51 cm); up to 4' wingspan

Male: White with gray wings, black wing tips spotted with white, and a white tail, seen in flight (inset). Yellow bill with a black ring near the tip. Yellowish legs and feet. In winter, the back of the head and the nape of the neck are speckled brown.

Female: same as male

Juvenile: white with brown speckles and a brown tip of tail; mostly dark bill

Nest: ground; female and male construct; 1 brood per year

Eggs: 2–4; off-white with brown markings

Incubation: 20–21 days; female and male incubate

Fledging: 20–40 days; female and male feed the young

Migration: partial to non-migrator

Food: insects, fish; scavenges for food

Compare: California Gull (p. 311) is larger and has a larger bill with a red-and-black mark near the tip; it also has dark eyes, compared with Ring-billed's light-colored eyes.

Stan's Notes: A common gull of garbage dumps and parking lots. Nests in Washington, sometimes nesting in mixed colonies with other gull species. Hundreds of these birds often flock together. A three-year gull with different plumages in each of its first three years. Attains the ring on its bill after the first winter and adult plumage in the third year. Defends a small area around the nest, usually only a few feet.

winter

juvenile

breeding

in flight

California Gull
Larus californicus

Size: 21" (53 cm); up to 4½' wingspan

Male: White bird with gray wings and black wing tips. A red-and-black mark on the tip of a yellow bill. Red ring around dark eyes. Winter or non-breeding adult has brown streaks on back of head and nape of neck.

Female: same as male

Juvenile: all brown for the first two years, similar to winter adult by the third year

Nest: ground; female and male construct; 1 brood per year

Eggs: 2–5; pale brown or olive, brown markings

Incubation: 24–26 days; female and male incubate

Fledging: 40–45 days; female and male feed young

Migration: partial migrator to complete, along western coastal U.S. and Mexico; non-migrator in parts of Washington

Food: insects, seeds, mammals

Compare: Ring-billed Gull (p. 309) is smaller and lacks California Gull's dark eyes and red mark on bill.

YEAR-ROUND
MIGRATION
WINTER

Stan's Notes: A four-year gull that appears nearly all brown during the first two years. Third-year bird is similar to the winter adult. Usually doesn't nest until the fourth year, when it obtains adult plumage. Nests in large colonies of up to 1,000 nests in Washington. Moves to the coast for the winter. Named for its usual winter sites along the California coast. Common on reservoirs.

winter

in flight

breeding

Caspian Tern
Sterna caspia

SUMMER
MIGRATION

Size: 21" (53 cm); up to 4' wingspan

Male: White chest and belly. Light-gray back. White wing surfaces below and light gray above, with black tips, as seen in flight. Black cap extends over eyes. Large dark-red bill with darker tip. Black legs. Winter plumage has a streaked cap.

Female: same as male

Juvenile: similar to winter adult, orange bill

Nest: ground; female and male construct; 1 brood per year

Eggs: 1–4; pinkish with brown markings

Incubation: 20–22 days; female and male incubate

Fledging: 30–40 days; female and male feed the young

Migration: complete, to coastal California and Mexico

Food: fish, aquatic insects

Compare: Smaller and more streamlined than most gulls, with thinner wings than gull wings. Look for the large red bill and black cap.

Stan's Notes: A large strong tern with a deep, harsh loud scream. Has been expanding in western Washington over the past 40 years. Frequently seen in large groups flying at about 30 feet (9 m) above water, patrolling for fish. Nests in large colonies on small islands and sand beaches. The young recognize the calls of their parents, which helps them find each other when adults return to the colony with food. Young chase adults until they are fed. Adults feed young for up to seven months, the longest time of any tern species.

313

in flight

breeding

juvenile

winter

Herring Gull
Larus argentatus

MIGRATION
WINTER

Size: 23–26" (58–66 cm); up to 5' wingspan

Male: White with slate-gray wings. Black wing tips with tiny white spots. Yellow bill with an orange-red spot near the tip of the lower bill (mandible). Pinkish legs and feet. Winter plumage has gray speckles on head and neck.

Female: same as male

Juvenile: mottled brown to gray, with a black bill

Nest: ground; female and male construct; 1 brood per year

Eggs: 2–3; olive with brown markings

Incubation: 24–28 days; female and male incubate

Fledging: 35–36 days; female and male feed the young

Migration: complete, to entire west coast from Canada to Mexico

Food: fish, insects, clams, eggs, baby birds

Compare: Ring-billed Gull (p. 309) is smaller and has yellowish legs and feet and a black ring on its bill. Look for the orange-red spot on the bill to help identify the Herring Gull.

Stan's Notes: A common gull of large lakes. An opportunistic bird, scavenging for human food in dumpsters, parking lots and other places with garbage. Takes eggs and young from other bird nests. Often drops clams and other shellfish from heights to break the shells and get to the soft interior. Nests in colonies, returning to the same site annually. Lines its nest with grass and seaweed. It takes about four years for the juveniles to obtain adult plumage. Adults have spotted heads during winter.

non-breeding in flight

breeding in flight

winter

juvenile

juvenile in flight

Glaucous-winged Gull
Larus glaucescens

YEAR-ROUND
WINTER

Size: 26" (66 cm); up to 4¾' wingspan

Male: White gull with a light-gray back and wings, with white spots on wing tips. Yellow bill with red spot on the lower bill. Dark eyes with a pink eye-ring around each eye. Pink legs. Winter plumage has a brown-streaked head and neck.

Female: same as male

Juvenile: gray to brown overall with a black bill

Nest: ground; female and male construct; 1 brood per year

Eggs: 1–3; olive with brown markings

Incubation: 27–29 days; female and male incubate

Fledging: 35–55 days; female and male feed young

Migration: non-migrator to partial migrator, along western coastal U.S. and Mexico

Food: insects, fish, shellfish, garbage

Compare: Herring Gull (p. 315) is similar in size and color, but it has black-tipped wings.

Stan's Notes: A four-year gull, taking four years to reach maturity. Starts out entirely gray to brown. Second-year gull is light gray with patches of white. Third-year gull resembles the winter adult, with a brown-streaked head and neck, white body and gray back and wings. Fourth-year gull has breeding plumage. Returns to the same nesting colony each year, often breeding with mate from previous year. Male bends forward and pops head up while calling for mate. Hybridizes with Herring Gulls.

blue morph

juvenile

white
morph

in flight

Snow Goose

Chen caerulescens

MIGRATION
WINTER

Size: 25–38" (64–97 cm); up to 4½' wingspan

Male: White morph has black wing tips and varying patches of black and brown. Blue morph has a white head and a gray breast and back. Both morphs have a pink bill and legs.

Female: same as male

Juvenile: overall dull gray with a dark bill

Nest: ground; female builds; 1 brood per year

Eggs: 3–5; white without markings

Incubation: 23–25 days; female incubates

Fledging: 45–49 days; female and male teach the young to feed

Migration: complete, to parts of Washington, Oregon, California and Arizona

Food: aquatic insects and plants

Compare: The Canada Goose (p. 267) is larger and has a black neck and white chin strap.

Stan's Notes: This bird occurs in light (white) and dark (blue) color morphs. The white morph is more common than the blue. A bird of wide-open fields, wetlands and lakes of any size. It has a thick, serrated bill, which helps it to grab and pull up plants. Breeds in large colonies on the northern tundra in Canada. Female starts to breed at 2–3 years. Older females produce more eggs and are more successful at reproduction than younger females. Seen by the thousands during migration and in winter. Commonly seen with Sandhill Cranes. Has a classic goose-like call.

in flight

Great Egret
Ardea alba

Size: 36–40" (91–102 cm); up to 4½' wingspan

Male: Tall, thin, all-white bird with a long neck and a long, pointed yellow bill. Black, stilt-like legs and black feet.

Female: same as male

Juvenile: same as adults

Nest: platform; male and female construct; 1 brood per year

Eggs: 2–3; light blue without markings

Incubation: 23–26 days; female and male incubate

Fledging: 43–49 days; female and male feed the young

Migration: complete, to southern states, Mexico and Central America; non-migrator in parts of the state

Food: small fish, aquatic insects, frogs, crayfish

Compare: The Great Blue Heron (p. 269) is larger in size but has a similar shape. Look for the Great Egret's all-white body, black legs and yellow bill.

Stan's Notes: Slowly stalks shallow ponds, lakes and wetlands in search of small fish to spear with its long, sharp bill. Gives a loud, dry croak if disturbed or when squabbling for a nest site at the colony. The name "Egret" comes from the French word *aigrette,* meaning "ornamental tufts of plumes." The plumes grow near the tail during the breeding season. Hunted to near extinction in the 1800s and early 1900s for its long plumes, which were used to decorate women's hats. Today, the egret is a protected species.

female

male

Wilson's Warbler
Cardellina pusilla

SUMMER
MIGRATION

Size: 4¾" (12 cm)

Male: Dull-yellow upper and bright-yellow lower. Distinctive black cap. Large black eyes and small thin bill.

Female: same as male, but lacking the black cap

Juvenile: similar to female

Nest: cup; female builds; 1 brood per year

Eggs: 4–6; white with brown markings

Incubation: 10–13 days; female incubates

Fledging: 8–11 days; female and male feed young

Migration: complete, to Mexico and Central America

Food: insects

Compare: Yellow Warbler (p. 331) is brighter yellow with orange streaking on the male's chest. Male American Goldfinch (p. 325) has a black forehead and black wings. The male Common Yellowthroat (p. 327) has a very distinctive black mask.

Stan's Notes: A widespread warbler of low to mid-level elevations west of the Cascades. Can be found near water in willow and alder thickets. Its all-insect diet makes it one of the top insect-eating birds in North America. Often flicks its tail and spreads its wings when hopping among thick shrubs, looking for insects. Females often mate with males that have the best territories and that might already have mates (polygyny).

male

winter male

female

American Goldfinch
Spinus tristis

YEAR-ROUND

Size: 5" (13 cm)

Male: Canary-yellow finch with a black forehead and tail. Black wings with white wing bars. White rump. No markings on the chest. Winter male is similar to the female.

Female: dull olive-yellow plumage with brown wings; lacks a black forehead

Juvenile: same as female

Nest: cup; female builds; 1 brood per year

Eggs: 4–6; pale blue without markings

Incubation: 10–12 days; female incubates

Fledging: 11–17 days; female and male feed the young

Migration: partial migrator to non-migrator; small flocks of up to 20 birds move around North America to find food

Food: seeds, insects; will come to seed feeders

Compare: The Pine Siskin (p. 99) and female House Finch (p. 101) both have a streaked chest. Male Yellow Warbler (p. 331) is all yellow with orange streaks on the chest. The male Wilson's Warbler (p. 323) lacks black wings.

Stan's Notes: A common backyard resident. Most often found in open fields, scrubby areas and woodlands. Enjoys Nyjer seed in feeders. Lines its nest with the silky down from wild thistle. Almost always in small flocks. Twitters while it flies. Flight is roller coaster-like. Often called Wild Canary due to the male's canary-colored plumage. Male sings a pleasant, high-pitched song.

Common Yellowthroat
Geothlypis trichas

SUMMER

Size: 5" (13 cm)

Male: Olive-brown with a bright-yellow throat and chest, a white belly and a distinctive black mask outlined in white. Long, thin, pointed black bill.

Female: similar to male but lacks a black mask

Juvenile: same as female

Nest: cup; female builds; 2 broods per year

Eggs: 3–5; white with brown markings

Incubation: 11–12 days; female incubates

Fledging: 10–11 days; female and male feed the young

Migration: complete, to southern California, Mexico and Central America

Food: insects

Compare: The male American Goldfinch (p. 325) has a black forehead and wings. Male Yellow Warbler (p. 331) has fine orange streaks on chest and lacks the black mask. The Yellow-rumped Warbler (p. 229) only has patches of yellow and lacks the yellow chest of the Yellowthroat. Male Wilson's Warbler (p. 323) lacks the male Yellowthroat's black mask.

Stan's Notes: A common warbler of open fields and marshes. Sings a cheerful, well-known "witchity-witchity-witchity-witchity" song from deep within tall grasses. Male sings from prominent perches and while he hunts. He performs a curious courtship display, bouncing in and out of tall grass while singing a mating song. Female builds a nest low to the ground. Young remain dependent on their parents longer than most other warblers. A frequent cowbird host.

Orange-crowned Warbler
Oreothlypis celata

SUMMER
MIGRATION

Size: 5" (13 cm)

Male: An overall pale-yellow bird with a dark line through eyes. Faint streaking on sides and chest. Tawny-orange crown, often invisible. Small thin bill.

Female: same as male, but very slightly duller, often indistinguishable in the field

Juvenile: same as adults

Nest: cup; female builds; 1–2 broods per year

Eggs: 3–6; white with brown markings

Incubation: 12–14 days; female incubates

Fledging: 8–10 days; female and male feed young

Migration: complete, to California, Mexico and Central America

Food: insects, fruit, nectar

Compare: Yellow Warbler (p. 331) is brighter yellow with orange streaking on the male's chest. Male Common Yellowthroat (p. 327) has a distinctive black mask. Wilson's Warbler (p. 323) is brighter yellow with a distinct black cap.

Stan's Notes: A widespread bird across the state. A nesting resident but often seen more during migration when large groups move together. Builds a bulky, well-concealed nest on the ground with nest rim at ground level. Known to feed at sapsucker taps and drink flower nectar. The orange crown tends to be hidden and is rarely seen in the field. A widespread breeder, from western Texas to Alaska and across Canada and south to California.

male

female

Yellow Warbler
Setophaga petechia

SUMMER

Size: 5" (13 cm)

Male: Yellow with thin orange streaks on the chest and belly. Long, pointed, dark bill.

Female: same as male but lacks orange streaks

Juvenile: similar to female but much duller

Nest: cup; female builds; 1 brood per year

Eggs: 4–5; white with brown markings

Incubation: 11–12 days; female incubates

Fledging: 10–12 days; female and male feed the young

Migration: complete, to California, Mexico, and Central and South America

Food: insects

Compare: Orange-crowned Warbler (p. 329) is paler yellow. The male American Goldfinch (p. 325) has a black forehead and black wings. The female American Goldfinch (p. 325) has white wing bars. Similar to male Wilson's Warbler (p. 323), which has a black cap, and lacks orange streaks on chest and belly. Look for the orange streaks on the chest to identify the male Yellow Warbler.

Stan's Notes: A common and widespread warbler in Washington. Seen in shrubby areas close to water, gardens and backyards. Zooms around shrubs and shorter trees. A prolific insect eater, gleaning caterpillars and other insects from tree leaves. Male sings a string of notes that sound like "sweet, sweet, sweet, I'm-so-sweet!" Begins to migrate south in August; returns in late April. Males arrive in spring before females to claim territories. Migrates at night in mixed flocks of warblers. Rests and feeds during the day.

331

male
p. 303

female

YEAR-ROUND
WINTER

Red Crossbill
Loxia curvirostra

Size: 6½" (16 cm)

Female: A pale yellow-gray sparrow-sized bird with a pale-yellow chest and light-gray patch on the throat. Long, pointed, crossed bill. Dark-brown wings and a short dark-brown tail.

Male: dirty-red to orange with a bright-red crown and rump, a crossed bill, dark-brown wings and a short dark-brown tail

Juvenile: streaked with tinges of yellow, bill gradually crosses about 2 weeks after fledging

Nest: cup; female builds; 1 brood per year

Eggs: 3–4; bluish white with brown markings

Incubation: 14–18 days; female incubates

Fledging: 16–20 days; female and male feed young

Migration: non-migrator to irruptive; moves around the state in winter in search of food

Food: seeds, leaf buds; comes to seed feeders

Compare: Similar in shape and size to female Purple Finch (p. 117). Female American Goldfinch (p. 325) is smaller. Look for the unique crossed bill to help identify.

Stan's Notes: The long crossed bill is adapted for extracting seeds from pine and spruce cones, its favorite food. Often dangles upside down like a parrot to reach cones. Plumage can be highly variable among individuals. Nests in coniferous forests at any elevation, mainly west of the Cascades. Migrating crossbills from farther north move to the state in winter, searching for food, swelling populations. This irruptive behavior makes it more common in some winters and nonexistent in others.

male

non-breeding male

female

Western Tanager
Piranga ludoviciana

SUMMER
MIGRATION

Size: 7¼" (18.5 cm)

Male: A canary-yellow bird with a red head. Black back, tail, wings. One white and one yellow wing bar. Non-breeding lacks the red head.

Female: duller than male, lacking the red head

Juvenile: similar to female

Nest: cup; female builds; 1 brood per year

Eggs: 3–5; light blue with brown markings

Incubation: 14–18 days; female incubates

Fledging: 16–20 days; female and male feed young

Migration: complete, to Mexico and Central America

Food: insects, fruit

Compare: The unique coloring makes the breeding male Tanager easy to identify. Male American Goldfinch (p. 325) has a black forehead. Female Bullock's Oriole (p. 337) lacks the female Tanager's single yellow wing bars.

Stan's Notes: Most common in the western half of the state. The male Western Tanager has stunning breeding plumage. Feeds mainly on insects, such as bees, wasps, cicadas and grasshoppers, and to a lesser degree on fruit. The male feeds the female while she incubates. Female builds a cup nest in a horizontal fork of a coniferous tree, well away from the main trunk, 20–40 feet (6–12 m) aboveground. This is the farthest-nesting tanager species, reaching far up into the Northwest Territories of Canada. An early fall migrant, often seen migrating in late July (when non-breeding males lack red heads). Seen in many habitats during migration.

male
p. 291

female

Bullock's Oriole
Icterus bullockii

Size: 8" (20 cm)

Female: Dull-yellow head and chest. Gray-to-black wings with white wing bars. A pale-white belly. Gray back, as seen in flight.

Male: bright-orange-and-black bird with a bold white patch on wings

Juvenile: similar to female

Nest: pendulous; female and male build; 1 brood per year

Eggs: 4–6; pale white to gray, brown markings

Incubation: 12–14 days; female incubates

Fledging: 12–14 days; female and male feed young

Migration: complete, to Central and South America

Food: insects, berries, nectar; visits nectar feeders

Compare: The only oriole that comes to Washington regularly. Smaller female Western Tanager (p. 335) has a black back, unlike female Bullock's gray back. Look for the female Bullock's dull-yellow and gray appearance.

Stan's Notes: So closely related to Baltimore Orioles of the eastern U.S., at one time both were considered a single species. Interbreeds with Baltimores where their ranges overlap. Most common in the state where cottonwood trees grow along rivers and other wetlands. Also found at edges of clearings, in city parks, on farms and along irrigation ditches. Hanging sock-like nest is constructed of plant fibers such as inner bark of junipers and willows. Will incorporate yarn and thread into its nest if offered at the time of nest building.

male

female

juvenile

Evening Grosbeak

Coccothraustes vespertinus

YEAR-ROUND
WINTER

Size: 8" (20 cm)

Male: Striking bird with bright-yellow eyebrows, rump and belly. Black-and-white wings and tail. Dark, dirty-yellow head and large, thick ivory-to-greenish bill.

Female: similar to male, with softer colors and a gray head and throat

Juvenile: similar to female, with a brown bill

Nest: cup; female builds; 1 brood per year

Eggs: 3–4; blue with brown markings

Incubation: 12–14 days; female incubates

Fledging: 13–14 days; female and male feed young

Migration: non-migrator to irruptive; moves around the state to find food

Food: seeds, insects, fruit; comes to seed feeders

Compare: The American Goldfinch (p. 325) is closely related, but it is much smaller. Look for the yellow eyebrows and thick bill to identify the Evening Grosbeak.

Stan's Notes: One of the largest finches. Characteristic finch-like undulating flight. Uses its unusually large bill to crack seeds, its main food source. Often seen on gravel roads eating gravel, which provides minerals, salt and grit to grind the seeds it eats. A year-round resident, it is more obvious during the winter because it moves in large flocks, searching for food, often coming to feeders. Sheds the outer layer of its bill during spring, exposing a blue-green bill.

Western Kingbird
Tyrannus verticalis

SUMMER

Size: 9" (22.5 cm)

Male: Bright-yellow belly and yellow under wings. Gray head and chest, often with white chin. Wings and tail are dark gray to nearly black with white outer edges on tail.

Female: same as male

Juvenile: similar to adult, less yellow and more gray

Nest: cup; female and male construct; 1 brood per year

Eggs: 3–4; white with brown markings

Incubation: 18–20 days; female incubates

Fledging: 16–18 days; female and male feed young

Migration: complete, to Mexico and Central America

Food: insects, berries

Compare: The Eastern Kingbird (p. 235) lacks any yellow of the Western Kingbird. Western Meadowlark (p. 343) also shares the yellow belly of Western Kingbird, but it has a distinctive black V-shaped necklace.

Stan's Notes: A bird of open country, frequently seen sitting on top of the same shrub or fence post. Hunts by watching for crickets, bees, grasshoppers and other insects and flying out to catch them, then returns to perch. Parents teach young how to hunt, bringing wounded insects back to the nest for the young to chase. Returns in April. Builds nest in May, often in a fork of a small single trunk tree. More common in eastern half of the state, where nearly every stand of trees around a homestead or farm is home to a pair of Western Kingbirds.

Western Meadowlark
Sturnella neglecta

YEAR-ROUND
SUMMER

Size: 9" (22.5 cm)

Male: Heavy-bodied bird with a short tail. Yellow chest and brown back. Prominent V-shaped black necklace. White outer tail feathers.

Female: same as male

Juvenile: same as adult

Nest: cup, on the ground in dense cover; female builds; 2 broods per year

Eggs: 3–5; white with brown markings

Incubation: 13–15 days; female incubates

Fledging: 11–13 days; female and male feed young

Migration: partial to non-migrator in Washington

Food: insects, seeds

Compare: Western Kingbird (p. 341) shares the yellow belly, but it lacks the V-shaped black necklace. Look for a black V marking on the chest to help identify the Meadowlark.

Stan's Notes: Most common in open country in the eastern part of the state. Named "Meadowlark" because it's a bird of meadows and sings like the larks of Europe. Best known for its wonderful song—a flute-like, clear whistle. Often seen perching on fence posts but quickly dives into tall grass when approached. Conspicuous white marks on sides of tail, seen when flying away. Not in the lark family; a blackbird family member and is related to grackles and orioles. Overall population is down greatly due to agricultural activities and ditch mowing.

BIRDING ON THE INTERNET

Birding online is a great way to discover additional information and learn more about birds. These websites will assist you in your pursuit of birds. Web addresses sometimes change a bit, so if one no longer works, just enter the name of the group into a search engine to track down the new address.

Site	Address
Author Stan Tekiela's homepage	naturesmart.com
American Birding Association	aba.org
Audubon Washington	wa.audubon.org
The Cornell Lab of Ornithology	birds.cornell.edu
eBird	ebird.org
Northwest Raptor & Wildlife Center	nwraptorcenter.com
Washington Ornithological Society	wos.org

CHECKLIST/INDEX BY SPECIES

Use the boxes to check the birds you've seen.

MORE FOR WASHINGTON BY STAN TEKIELA

Birding Guides

Birds of Prey of the West
Field Guide

Birds of the Northwest

Pacific Northwest Birding
Companion

Stan Tekiela's Birding for
Beginners: Pacific Northwest

Nature Books

Bird Trivia

Start Mushrooming

A Year in Nature with Stan Tekiela

**Children's Books:
Adventure Board Book Series**

Floppers & Loppers

Paws & Claws

Peepers & Peekers

Snouts & Sniffers

Children's Books

C is for Cardinal

Can You Count the Critters?

Critter Litter

**Children's Books:
Wildlife Picture Books**

Baby Bear Discovers the World

The Cutest Critter

Do Beavers Need Blankets?

Hidden Critters

Jump, Little Wood Ducks

Some Babies Are Wild

Super Animal Powers

What Eats That?

Whose Baby Butt?

Whose Butt?

Whose House Is That?

Whose Track Is That?

OBSERVATION NOTES

ABOUT THE AUTHOR

Naturalist, wildlife photographer and writer Stan Tekiela is the originator of the popular state-specific field guide series that includes the *Birds of Prey of the West Field Guide*. Stan has authored more than 190 educational books, including field guides, quick guides, nature books, children's books, and more, presenting many species of animals and plants.

With a Bachelor of Science degree in natural history from the University of Minnesota and as an active professional naturalist for more than 30 years, Stan studies and photographs wildlife throughout the United States and Canada. He has received national and regional awards for his books and photographs and is also a well-known columnist and radio personality. His syndicated column appears in more than 25 newspapers, and his wildlife programs are broadcast on a number of Midwest radio stations. You can follow Stan on Facebook and Twitter or contact him via his website, naturesmart.com.